IDEAS TO SAVE

YOUR LIFE

THE 15-MINUTE
ECONOMIST

D1210249

ARCTURUS

ARCTURUS

This edition published in 2016 by Arcturus Publishing Limited
26/27 Bickels Yard, 151–153 Bermondsey Street,
London SE1 3HA

ISBN: 978-1-78404-654-5
AD004461UK

Printed in China

Contents

What is economics about?

Would you rather go on holiday or buy a new sofa? Would you prefer your government to spend more on education or reduce taxes? Should healthcare be free?

Questions like these lie at the heart of economics. They require us to choose how to use the financial resources available to us or our government, knowing that choosing one thing often means giving up another. They arise when we have to deal with scarcity – with choosing how to allocate limited resources.

These questions come about because for most people – and all governments – money is a limited resource. You might not have enough money to buy both a sofa and a holiday. A government might not have enough money to improve education and reduce taxes. It is not only about money; land and time are also limited resources. A farmer might not have enough land to keep both sheep and chickens.

If there were plenty of everything – unlimited food, land, housing, healthcare, education, transport, books – there would be no need for money, no need to choose or prioritize one thing over another, and consequently no need for economics. Economics arises from the need to choose how to spend what we have, to apportion our resources – to economize, in fact.

Never enough

All the things we use – the food, housing and books – are called **resources** by economists. Most of them are in limited supply; they are, in economics-speak, **scarce resources**. Economists use 'scarce' in a slightly different way from everyone else. They don't mean the resource is rare or in short supply in the way that snow leopards are scarce. They mean simply that the supply of the resource is limited: either it is not renewable, or it is not renewable at the rate at which it is used. So oil is a scarce resource, even though in some countries there is plenty of it, because eventually it will run out and cannot be replenished. Economics is, essentially, the process of making choices about how to use scarce resources.

A very few things are essentially unlimited in their supply. Examples are air, sea water, sunlight and wind power. Economists generally call these **free goods**, though in reality there is a limit to air and sea water.

How to choose

Scarcity forces us to make choices. This is true at all levels: we make choices as individual consumers, businesses make choices and so do governments. You or I might choose whether to use our time maintaining a vegetable garden or playing a sport; we have limited time and have to choose how best to use it.

A business might choose whether to use its limited number of staff to make wheelbarrows or to make ladders, according to which it thinks will be more profitable. A government might choose whether to spend more on welfare payments or on road-building.

In each case, we have to weigh up the **costs** and **benefits** of each possibility. There is often a **trade-off**: this generally means that having one thing requires us to relinquish another thing. If you spend your money on a holiday,

NO LIMITS

Free goods can be produced with no cost in terms of resources. Ironically, this leads to a definition of free goods that can include or exclude identical items. Intangible goods such as a computer program, web page or ebook that can be downloaded any number of times without using more resources are free goods. The original composition, though, took resources to create (in the form of time, skill and effort). If a publisher makes a charge for the program or ebook, identical copies of the item are no longer a free good because the consumer has to use resources (money) to acquire them. Intellectual property rights convert a free good to a scarce good in recognition of the resources used in its original creation.

you may not have enough to spend on new furniture. If you work part-time in order to spend more time with your family, you will earn less money than if you worked full-time. You can choose to have (or give up) either money or free time.

Lost and costly opportunities

Economists apply mathematics to these commonplace ideas, making it possible to create useful models that can explain what happens in an economy and help individuals, businesses and governments to make plans for the future.

Imagine a farmer who can grow both strawberries and raspberries on her land. She only has a limited amount of land, so must decide the most profitable way of using it.

If the farmer chooses to grow more strawberries she must grow fewer raspberries, and vice versa. If we draw a graph, we can calculate the opportunity cost of growing each fruit. She just has three polytunnels, so she must choose how many to allocate to strawberries and how many to raspberries.

If she decides to use two polytunnels for strawberries, she then has only one polytunnel to grow raspberries. For each polytunnel of strawberries she grows, the opportunity cost is one polytunnel of raspberries, and for each polytunnel of raspberries she grows, the opportunity cost is one polytunnel of strawberries.

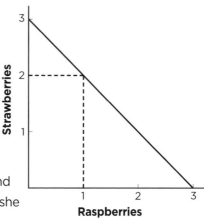

The curve gets curvy

In this case, the opportunity-cost graph is a straight line: each polytunnel of strawberries costs one polytunnel of raspberries and vice versa. But it is rarely this straightforward. Here's another example: suppose we have an island that has rich, fertile land at one end and rocky scrubland at the other end. The principal farming products of the island are goats and wheat. The islanders have to decide how to allocate the land. This time, the opportunity cost is not a straight line because the resource (land) is uneven. It will be very difficult to grow wheat on the rocky scrubland – little will take root there. But goats can tolerate scrubland. It is also easy to keep goats on the fertile land, but that would be a waste as it is good for growing wheat.

The islanders would begin by growing wheat on the fertile land. As they ran out of fertile land, the yield of wheat per acre would drop.

On the rocky scrubland, the yield would be low. This means that the opportunity cost involved in growing wheat rises as they are forced to use less suitable land. They might need to displace one goat per

400kg of wheat on the fertile land, but four goats to gain 400kg of wheat on the scrubland. The opportunity cost of 400kg of wheat therefore varies between one and four goats. Conversely, the opportunity cost of keeping a goat on the

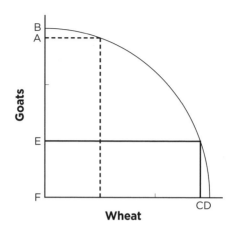

fertile land is 400kg of wheat, but the opportunity cost of keeping a goat on the scrubland is only 400 ÷ 4 = 100kg of wheat.

The graph shows that the opportunity cost in goats of the first crop of wheat is low, just AB. As we move further along the curve, using ever more unsuitable land for growing wheat, the opportunity cost rises. The small yield of wheat represented by CD comes at the cost of a lot of potential goats (EF). The largest total production (of goats and wheat together) comes somewhere in the middle of the curve. This represents the point at which the best land is used to produce wheat and the worst land is used to produce goats. It is the most productive use of resources. At this point, the economy is as successful as it can be in this scenario.

More and less: supply and demand

The simple graph of the fruit farmer's opportunity cost in growing strawberries and raspberries gives her no way of choosing which crop to grow except personal preference. In fact, there will be other factors to consider. She might be concerned that if she produces just one crop not enough people will want to buy it. In economic terms, this means she must decide whether there will be sufficient **demand** for (say) raspberries to ensure the entire **supply** is sold. If demand is low, she will have to sell raspberries for a lower price to get rid of them. Otherwise there's a danger she won't sell them before they rot. She might decide it is safer and more profitable to split her resources

WORKING AT THE FRONTIERS

The curve showing how a country can divide its resources between wheat and goats is called a **production possibility frontier** (PPF) curve. If a nation produces at any point along the curve then all its resources are in use. If it produces inside the curve (to the left of the line), it has unused resources and is less productive than it could be – there is room for improvement. It can only produce at a point outside (to the right) of the curve if circumstances change. Perhaps farmers start planting wheat with a higher yield or a variety that tolerates poorer quality soil, or maybe they increase plot yield by applying more fertilizer.

(polytunnels, fertilizer, farm workers) between two crops. It increases the likelihood that she will sell all her produce, and she may even be able to charge a higher price for it if demand is high compared with the supply. Supply and demand are central to shaping an economy (see page 44 – *How do supply and demand work?*).

Wants and needs

Consumers, those who buy or 'consume' goods and services, use their resources to get the things they **need** and also the things they **want**. As long as they have enough money to buy everything they need, they can use what is left over to buy the things they want. In economics, the distinction between needs and wants is important.

Needs must be met in order for a person to survive. They include food and drink, shelter and sufficient clothes to keep us warm. These are our most basic needs. Other needs vary according to time and place. For example, Scandinavians need lots of warm clothes, whereas someone living in Niger does not.

Items considered necessary vary between cultures and change over time. In the modern world, a car might be considered a necessity in rural areas as it would be difficult to get around without one. In the past, a horse was a necessity, but now it is a luxury. Economists put some effort into deciding what someone believes they need in order to have an acceptable standard of living.

Once basic needs have been met, any surplus money can be spent on meeting wants. Unlike needs, wants are limitless. We only need a certain amount of food, and sufficient shelter and clothing to protect us from the weather, but our wants go on and on. Once we have enough food, we might want tastier food. We might want a larger house, a better car, more holidays, more fashionable clothes – there is no end to what people want. All but the very wealthiest people have to decide how to allocate their money, choosing which 'wants' should be met and which not. Even the wealthiest have to make choices about how to spend their time, as we all have a limited lifespan – there is not time to do everything.

For the farmer who grows raspberries and strawberries, it's necessary to make the fruit appealing because consumers don't *need* either. (Although they need food, they don't necessarily need these particular types of food.) People might choose to spend money on these rather than on other luxury food items, such as ice cream, or on other fruit, such as apples. One thing that will determine how consumers spend their money is price.

In the market

When economists use the term **market**, they don't just mean a collection of open-air stalls. They mean anywhere – real or virtual – where buyers and sellers interact to exchange goods and services for money. They talk about 'markets' for different goods and services. There is, for instance, a market for electricity and a market for motorbikes. There are usually many sellers and many buyers. The sellers try to attract buyers, competing with other sellers in the same market by offering more attractive prices, better quality products, and so on. There is also competition between markets, especially in the case of goods that satisfy wants rather than needs. While everyone must choose an electricity supplier, people may or may not buy a motorbike. Sellers of motorbikes not only have to compete with other types of transport, but also other leisure activities.

> **ECONOMICS-SPEAK: GOODS AND SERVICES**
>
> Consumers spend their money on **goods** and **services**. In simple terms, goods are physical items such as computers, bicycles, pies and bottles of beer. Services are activities carried out by other people as a service to the customer, such as cutting hair, cleaning windows, giving financial advice, serving a meal in a restaurant or mending a heating system.

How to make an economy

An economy only emerges when there are people who interact to **produce** and **exchange** goods and services. There are economies of all sizes: you have your own household economy; there is a wider local economy, and that is part of a national economy. The national economy is part of a global economy.

If we all lived isolated lives, growing all the food we ate, making our own clothes, building our own homes, looking after and educating our own children and dealing with our healthcare problems ourselves, there would be no economic activity. Economic activity emerges when people form societies and cooperate. With an economy, markets grow up for different goods and services, a means of exchange emerges (now money, but once it was **barter** – see page 21), and a need to allocate resources arises.

Economics deals with how people – individuals, societies and nations – allocate resources in order to produce the goods and services required to meet people's wants and needs. An economy faces three important questions:

- **What** will be produced? There are limited resources, so they have to be allocated with care.
- **How** will production be organized? There are different ways to make goods and deliver services. An economy will seek the most efficient methods of production to make the most of its resources.

MACRO AND MICRO

There are two broad categories of economics:

- **Microeconomics** is concerned with the economic activity and decisions of individuals and businesses. It covers issues such as choosing how to spend your money, dealing with taxes and investments, looking at prices and costs and so on.
- **Macroeconomics** is concerned with much broader issues, such as the economies of whole countries or of entire industries, like petrochemicals or agriculture. It looks at issues such as employment, inflation, interest rates, national wealth and exchange rates.

- **Who** will benefit from the goods and services produced? Some goods and services will be for public use and some for private use. The distribution of wealth in a society is related to this question.

These key questions are addressed in this book. Economics extends far beyond money markets and even beyond economies. Applied economics uses the principles of economics to investigate other situations where the same issues of supply and demand or allocation of resources are relevant, including ecology.

The limits of economics

Economics is not a science like physics, in which new theories can be proved or disproved through experimentation. Many of the issues touched on in this book remain open for discussion, and different economists often have opposing views about how they should be tackled or interpreted. Even when dealing with the most pressing

economic questions, such as how to save a failing national economy or combat famine in sub-Saharan Africa, economists wrangle over competing ideas and theories. Economics is a relatively new discipline and economies evolve and change rapidly. Economists haven't got it all right yet by a long way.

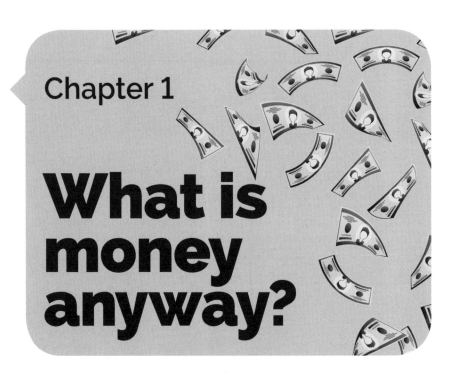

Chapter 1

What is money anyway?

Trade, or commerce (the buying and selling of goods and services) is a fundamental part of economics. And money is at the heart of commerce. It is familiar to us all, yet we rarely pause to think about what it really represents.

Money is any token, physical or virtual, that can be used in trade. Whatever is used as money might have intrinsic value, such as a disc of gold, or it might have only symbolic value, like a printed slip of paper with a fancy design. It might have no physical existence at all, like the virtual currency **bitcoin** – a digital currency that operates independently of the main banking system. Of course, even the 'intrinsic' value of a gold coin is culturally determined. Gold is of limited use outside jewellery and commerce. It is now used in electronics, but that use emerged long after gold was first considered valuable. It's easier to make crowns and jewellery from gold than other metals, as it's soft and doesn't corrode – but you could say the same of plastic. Crowns and jewellery, while nice, are not exactly essential to survival – they are not 'needs'.

Bartering doesn't go well

Try to imagine a world in which there is no form of money. If you want something you can't find or make yourself, you need to persuade someone who has it to give it to you. They will probably be unwilling to give it for free, but might be willing to swap it for something you have. This is called **bartering**. If you have a mammoth skin but want some watermelons, it might take a long time to find

GOLDEN CHAINS

The 16th-century philosopher Sir Thomas More satirized humankind's greed for gold in his book *Utopia*. The Utopians do not see value in gold, as it is virtually useless:

'Their chamber-pots and close-stools are made of gold and silver. . . . Of the same metals they also make chains and fetters for their slaves; on some of whom, as a badge of infamy, they hang an ear-ring of gold, and make others wear a chain or a coronet of the same metal. And thus they take care, by all possible means, to render gold and silver of no esteem. Hence it is that, while other countries part with these metals as though one tore-out their bowels, the Utopians would look upon giving-in all they had of them, when occasion required, as parting only with a trifle, or as we should esteem the loss of a penny.

'They find pearls on their coast, and diamonds and carbuncles on their rocks. They seek them not, but if they find them by chance, they polish them and give them to their children for ornaments, who delight in them during their childhood. But when they come to years of discretion, and see that none but children use such baubles, they lay them aside of their own accord; and would be as much ashamed to use them afterward, as grown children among us would be of their toys.'

Sir Thomas More, *Utopia*, Book 2 (1516)

someone with watermelons who wants a mammoth skin. If the person with watermelons wants a clay bowl, you might have to trade a mammoth skin for a clay bowl, and then trade that for watermelons – if you can even find someone with watermelons who wants a clay bowl. You can see how it quickly becomes a complex, time-consuming and often frustrating endeavour. This problem, called the **coincidence of wants**, or **double coincidence of wants**, makes bartering systems unwieldy and inefficient.

Instead, most societies have developed some form of exchange mechanism. This works on the basis that everyone agrees that some token (cowrie shells, perhaps) represents value. The value can be transferred between people and exchanged for goods and services. Now it's easy to trade a mammoth skin for cowrie shells and take the shells to someone who has watermelons. The watermelon farmer can use the cowrie shells to buy a chair or a boat or a chicken – whatever he or she needs. As everyone in the community accepts that cowrie shells have value, they become a means of exchange – or money.

The four functions of money

In 1875, the British economist William Jevons set out the four functions of money in his book *Money and the Mechanism of Exchange*. Money is, he said, a medium of exchange, a common measure of value, a standard

of value and a store of value. Some economists have argued that being a store of value and a medium of exchange are mutually exclusive, as storing it means you can't spend it (exchange), and spending it means you can't save it (storing). This is a trifle pedantic, as it has the potential to be both at different times.

A modern approach often lists three functions for money:
- a medium of exchange
- a store of value
- a unit of account.

It is called a **medium of exchange** as it facilitates the exchange (swapping) of goods and services, acting as an intermediary between disparate items such as mammoth skins and watermelons.

As a **store of value**, it's important that whatever is chosen as the means of exchange does not readily deteriorate or decay. This is one reason for choosing gold – it doesn't corrode, evaporate or change in any way over time, and it's difficult to destroy as it doesn't dissolve in most acids. It would not be sensible to choose, say, fresh fruit as a medium of exchange as it would soon rot.

Economists recognize two types of value: the **utility** (usefulness) of a particular good or service, and the **power** of a good or service when exchanged to acquire other goods and services. Anything used as money has exchange value. It can also have utility value, as we shall see.

The last function, a **unit of account**, means there must be a consistent way of measuring or counting money and that it provides the unit for pricing other items. This is served by currency: we count money in dollars, pounds, euro, yuan, yen, pesos and so on.

WHEN MONEY GOES WRONG

When an economy fails, prices may rise beyond all sensible measure and each unit of currency will then buy less and less – its exchange value falls. In this case, money itself is no longer a good store of value. The classic example of this is the period in the 1920s when the German currency, the mark, became virtually worthless. Something that cost one mark in 1918 cost three billion marks in 1923. As a result, some people in Germany began to use other currencies or media of exchange in preference to the mark (see page 180).

Commodity money

Physical items used as money are called **commodity money**. The item itself must have recognized intrinsic value. Examples of items that have been used as commodity money include:

- Buckskins and beaver pelts in North America. Hudson Bay had an official exchange rate for beaver pelts. One beaver pelt could be exchanged for two pairs of scissors, five pounds of sugar, 20 fish-hooks or a pair of shoes. Twelve beaver pelts would buy you a gun.

- Decorative items such as shells, mirrors, beads and decorated belts. Part of the payment that Dutch traders made to Native Americans when they bought Manhattan Island in 1626 was in beads, the total value of the goods traded being around 60 gilders ($1,000/£650).

- Axes. In 9th century Poland they were useful for cutting down trees and launching raids on neighbours.

- Bat and bird droppings (guano). The Incas used guano as a rich fertilizer.

- Food items which are slow to perish, such as salt,

THE ISLAND OF STONE MONEY

On the Pacific island of Yap, wheel-shaped stones have been used as money for centuries. Some are small, but others very large – up to 3.6m (12 ft) across and weighing over 4,000kg (4 tons). Made of limestone mined and carved in Palau, they were moved by bamboo canoe to Yap.

The agreed value of a stone depends on its size, craftsmanship and history. The most valuable stones, paradoxically, are those that killed no one in transit and those that killed most people in transit. They are so large and heavy that they are rarely moved; trade consists only of recording a change of ownership. One stone even fell into the sea during transport to Yap and was still traded because access to it was not important. Everyone knew where it was and who owned it, so ownership of the stone could change without the stone being moved. Ownership of a stone that can't be retrieved from the ocean is an early example of virtual money.

peppercorns, barley, rice, dried fish and cattle. Cattle are not divisible until dead, so rather inconvenient – a bit like an economy in which the only currency is $100 notes.

- Tobacco and cigarettes. Cigarettes have often been used by soldiers and prisoners as currency. A full economy based on cigarettes grew up in some prisoner-of-war camps in World War II. After smoking was banned in many US jails, foil pouches of mackerel fillets took over as the unit of currency.

Opportunity cost (see page 9) is clear with commodity money. The opportunity cost of paying for a stamp with a pouch of mackerel is the chance to eat the mackerel.

Modern money

For most of us, money is counted in units of a specific currency – dollars, pounds, euros, yen, yuan, lire, dinar and so on. This is called **fiat money** – the items exchanged have no intrinsic value, but they are agreed to have value for the sake of running the economy.

We are used to fiat money in the form of coins and notes, but increasingly also in virtual form. In the developed world today people are now less

THREE HEADS FOR THAT DRAGON JAR

Some of the Penan people in Borneo used the severed heads of their enemies as tributes to the spirits that had power over rice. Heads were offered to make the rice grow, but also became an item of value in their own right, because of their efficacy as spirit-bribes. There was no physical trade in heads, though, as trading them was considered unlucky. Instead, a head was equivalent to a living slave or captive, which could be traded. Some items had a value as 'virtual heads'. A dragon jar – a large receptacle with a green glaze and dragon motif, imported from China – was valued at three heads. If someone killed a person, requiring a tribute to the bereaved family of three heads, the debt could be discharged by the transfer of a dragon jar.

likely to be paid in cash. Their salary is more likely to be deposited in their bank as a figure that increases their balance, and is often spent by wielding a card that authorizes a business to reduce the balance, or by setting up a direct debit or standing order that lets them take away some of the balance on a regular basis. We might sometimes withdraw some cash – but for most of us today cash is not really the dominant form of money (see page 212 – *Is cash on the way out?*)

Two types of money

Increasingly, money has become dissociated from the real, physical world. I get paid for thinking and jiggling my fingers about over a keyboard. It's about as unreal as you can get. The money I get for it is paid straight into my bank account and the bank takes out chunks for the mortgage, utilities and so on at regular intervals. The rest I spend by waving a bit of plastic or clicking on web pages. At any point, I could, in theory, go and take all my money out of the bank as cash. In practice, I would be challenged at every step: they would assume I was going to do something illegal with it, since people don't usually withdraw all their money in this way. And it would be impossible to obtain my money if everyone else tried to draw

FROM COMMODITY TO FIAT AND BACK

Early Chinese coins had holes in them so that they could be strung on a thread or thong and were easy to keep. Since the coins had greater face value than the intrinsic value of the metal they were made from, they were an example of fiat money.

Chinese coins that came into the hands of tribespeople in parts of Malaysia were sometimes adopted as a local currency, but their value bore no relation to the face value of the coins. Instead, the holes made them useful as decorative items that could be fixed to other things, such as jewellery or head-dresses. The coins then became commodity money, based on their value as intrinsically useful items.

theirs out at the same time. This is because money is now largely theoretical and there is nowhere near as much cash in existence as there is 'money' in the economic system. The money that is held only as electronic records is called **bank money**, for fairly obvious reasons.

Bank money is used to move money between financial institutions, governments, large corporations and so on. If you pay $20 to a bookshop using a debit card, there is no physical movement of actual money between your bank and the bookshop's bank. The entire transaction, and all similar transactions, are carried out using bank money. In the UK, 97 per cent of money held by the public is in the form of bank deposits rather than as cash (2014 figure).

A run on the bank

In the film *Mary Poppins*, Michael, the young son of Mr Banks, is reluctant to deposit his money in a bank. When the bank manager snatches it, Michael demands back his tuppence (two old pennies, or 2d). The other customers, misunderstanding what is happening, assume the bank can't honour a young customer's demand for tuppence and a 'run' on the bank ensues – that is, everyone tries to withdraw their money at the same time. This is, in a nutshell, what causes a run on a bank: too many depositors want their money back all at once, and the bank can't honour all the debts. A run generally starts because of a loss of confidence in the bank, and then becomes a self-fulfilling prophecy. In fact, if at any point all customers tried to take all their money out of the banks, the banks would not be able to honour the deposits. Usually only a minority of people want their money at any one time and everyone else believes they could

get hold of it if they needed to, and so the illusion and the banking system are sustained.

Genuine bank runs are relatively rare. There was a run on the Montreal City and District Savings Bank in 1872 in Canada; there were bank runs in the USA during the Great Depression in the 1930s; and there were bank runs of a slightly different type on Northern Rock in the UK in 2007, Landsbanki in Iceland in 2008 and the Greek banks in 2015.

How much money is there?

To put it simply, bank money exists provided people believe in it. If we all stopped believing and wanted it in hard cash, the system would collapse because bank money isn't really there (depending on your definition of 'really'). There are different ways of talking about how much money there is and therefore about what constitutes 'really'. In the USA, the two most important measures of the money supply are M0 and M1. Other countries use similar measures, sometimes with additional categories.

ECONOMICS-SPEAK: ASSETS AND LIABILITIES

An **asset** is anything that can be owned and which produces value (money). Assets include houses, money in the bank, a promise from someone to pay you money, or a machine for making something.

A **liability** is the opposite of an asset. A liability is something that entails a cost or obligation to pay for something in money or by some other means. Liabilities include an outstanding mortgage on a house, or a promise to buy a present for someone or deliver a lecture for free.

Assets and liabilities are always equally matched: your mortgage liability is equivalent to the bank's asset – a claim on part of the value of your house. If you owe $200,000 (a liability), the bank has an asset of $200,000 of value in the house.

- M0 is the total stock of cash – coins and notes – held by individuals and in banks and bank reserves. There is about $5 trillion (£3.25 trillion) of M0 in the world.
- M1 includes M0 and assets that are easily converted into cash (such as bank deposits in 24-hour access accounts). M1 comes to around $25 trillion (£16.25 trillion).
- M2, includes M0 and M1, and also longer-term, less liquid assets such as money tied up in savings accounts. It comes to around $60 trillion (£39 trillion).

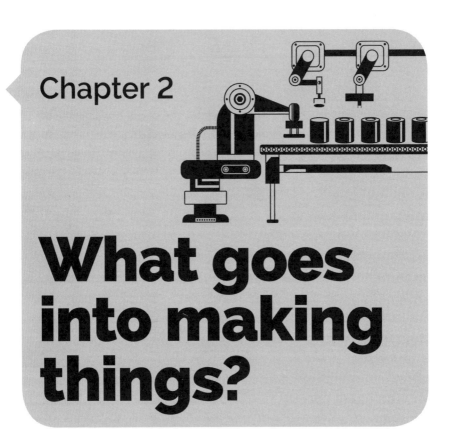

Chapter 2

What goes into making things?

Long ago, there were no manufactured goods.
Now, almost everything is processed in some way.

Our distant ancestors wandered the plains picking berries and roots and hunting animals that moved slowly enough to be killed easily.

At some point, they realized that sharpened stones and sticks could make catching animals easier, and making a fire to cook them made them tastier. The individual who invested time in sharpening a stone and making a spear was making an early form of economic decision: at the cost of time and labour (his or her own) and using a free resource (a stone and a stick), he or she made a manufactured good. The opportunity cost in making the spear was the time that could have been spent doing something else.

The utility of the spear (the benefit of the spear to the individual) was greater than the utility of the stone, stick and labour to make it, as it would secure food more easily and save time in the future. So making the spear added value; that is the defining feature of manufacturing industry.

Starting in business

An individual adept at making spears might also make them for other members of the group, perhaps in exchange for some skins to wear or some food to eat. A spear can have both *utility* value and *exchange* value.

In this example of early entrepreneurship, we can identify some of the basic elements of economic activity:

- the use of commodities: stones and sticks
- employing labour: the spear-maker's effort
- making manufactured goods: spears
- representing capital: spears
- increasing utility: the benefit of a spear
- providing revenue: meat and skins
- facilitating exchange: spears for skins or meat.

Factors of production

Economists talk of the **factors of production,** which go into producing any manufactured goods. Neoclassical economics considers there to be three factors of production: **land**, **capital** and **labour**.

Land not only covers the land itself but also anything on it, above it or drawn from within it. This means that natural resources such as trees growing on the land and oil underground also count as land. For the spear-maker, sticks and stones come from land.

Capital is everything that can be used in the production of goods to gain more goods. **Capital goods** are not used up in the manufacture of more items (though they might eventually wear out). In the modern world, capital includes large items, such as factory premises, machinery and vehicles (lorries and tractors, say), and small items, such as a gardener's tools and an artist's paintbrushes. For our early ancestor, the completed spear is a capital good, as it is used to secure food.

Labour is the work that people put in to make something. If you make something for yourself, your own effort is the labour involved. Often, people work for an employer – they sell their labour in exchange for **wages**. (Economists refer to 'wages' even when pay is a monthly salary or a one-off fee.) The early spear-maker uses his or her own labour.

NEOCLASSICAL ECONOMICS

Neoclassical economics is the dominant school of economic thought. It puts supply and demand and the individual's desire to maximize their profit or utility at the heart of economic activity. It uses mathematics and graphs extensively and bases its models on the belief that people will always act rationally. It has been criticized for this assumption, as people actually act in response to complex stimuli and biases and do not always (or even often) act with complete rationality. Neoclassical economics has been blamed for causing social inequality and poverty as it proposes that, given time, market forces will provide adequate workers' rights, and so on. Alternative approaches tend to be grouped together under the umbrella term **heterodox economics**.

Capital this and that

The traditional, narrow definition of capital – objects that are not used up in the production of goods – has been superseded in more recent economic thinking. Intangible forms of capital are now included, such as the skills of an individual trained to carry out a particular job, or the goodwill built up by a company through its dealings with customers and suppliers:

- **Financial capital** is money in the form of financial assets, including money in bank accounts, money loaned by investors and obligations by others to pay money.
- **Natural capital** is naturally occurring in the environment and is an enriching asset for everyone. Examples are trees, water and oil.

- **Human capital** covers all aspects of value in human talent, knowledge and social interactions. It includes some sub-categories, such as: *social capital,* characterized by human interactions that have value, such as brand loyalty and goodwill; *instructional capital*, or intellectual capital, is teaching or knowledge transfer – it can't be inherent in a single expert individual, but must be transferable; *individual capital* is the valuable skills, abilities and knowledge inherent in individuals – it is closely related to labour, and some economic approaches don't distinguish between the two.

The pioneering Scottish political economist Adam Smith distinguished between **fixed capital** – items not used up in production, such as tools and factories – and **circulating capital**, by which he meant items that are used up, such as raw materials.

The capital of a whole nation includes many goods from which everyone benefits, such as the infrastructure of roads and railways,

'That part of a man's stock which he expects to afford him revenue is called his capital.'
Adam Smith, *The Wealth of Nations* (1776)

amenities such as electricity and water supply, and publicly owned schools and hospitals.

Putting people at the centre: labour

Neoclassical economics does not make the people who provide labour (do the work) a particularly important part of the equation. It puts capital at the heart of economic activity. Workers are treated, in general, as a resource that can easily be replaced or renewed, with one working unit exchangeable for another.

The German political philosopher Karl Marx (1818–83), the author of *The Communist Manifesto*, saw production much more in terms of the use of labour than the use of capital. He defined the factors of production as **labour**, **subjects of labour**, and **instruments of labour**. Labour, again, is the individuals who do the work. The subjects of labour are the goods acted upon to make something (raw materials). In a coffee-processing plant, the coffee beans are the subjects of labour. The instruments of labour are the tools, buildings and machinery used to carry out the work (**capital assets**). In processing coffee beans, the roasters and other machines used are the instruments of labour. Marx put the value added by labour at the heart of the value of goods and services in an economy (see page 71). He considered all commodities to represent 'congealed labour'.

Sticks, stones and managers

The spear-maker who makes a spear for himself uses only freely available natural resources from the land and his own labour. If he collects a stock of suitable sticks and stones ready to make into spears, this collection would represent circulating capital, according to Adam Smith's definition.

Suppose now that an enterprising individual saw that the spear-maker was very good at making spears, but could only devote a short period of time to the task each day because of the need to do other things, such as catch and cook food, collect water and guard children from predators. This enterprising intermediary, or 'entrepreneur', might offer to take on one of these activities herself, in exchange for a share in the extra spears the spear-maker will now be able to produce. In fact, the 'entrepreneur' doesn't plan to guard the children herself. Instead she deposits them in the care of someone who is already occupied in minding children. It's no harder to keep predators away from four children than two – the cost to the 'childminder' in terms of additional effort is very low. The 'entrepreneur' gives away one spear to the 'childminder' to secure this service. Now the 'entrepreneur' has no tasks to perform, but has made a profit in terms of spears by acting as an intermediary between the manufacturer (spear-maker) and the service provider (childminder). This is something that modern economists call **entrepreneurial capital**. It is the management of an organization to make the 'best use' of its production.

Something for nothing?

In practice, although it looks as if the 'entrepreneur' does nothing, it's not quite nothing. She:

- sees an opportunity (or problem)
- thinks of a way of exploiting (or solving) it
- sources the different parties who can work together

- vets (we hope) the childminder
- handles the payment to the childminder
- oversees to ensure that the childminder does the work competently
- supervises the quality of the spears and rate of production.

While the spear-maker exploits natural capital (sticks and stones), the manager exploits human capital (spear-maker and childminder).

The entrepreneur might act as an agent, taking a percentage of the spears produced, or might act as an employer, perhaps even providing the sticks and stones and allowing the spear-maker to keep a certain number of the spears as a wage. In the last scenario, the entrepreneur has become a **capitalist** – someone who owns the means of production and puts it to use to make a profit, paying for labour in the process.

For all we know, there might have been enterprising managers or entrepreneurs long ago, but it is generally thought that this type of economic activity developed over time as western societies adopted more sophisticated forms of commerce (see page 92 – *How did we get here?*)

Chapter 3
How do supply and demand work?

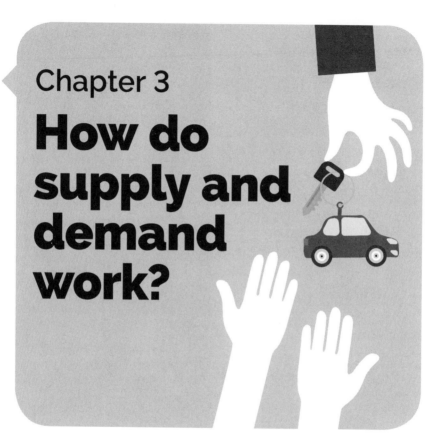

In a free market, economics follows the law of supply and demand.

Every economy works – or fails – by a process of supplying the goods, services and resources for which there is a demand. Supply and demand are therefore the main forces acting in an economy.

The demand curve

From everyday experience we know that demand for goods falls as price rises: you tend to buy less of something the more expensive it becomes. Economists show this relationship between the quantity people want and the price of an item by drawing a downward-sloping **demand curve**. (Although it's called a curve, it's usually a straight line.)

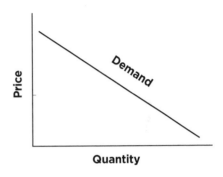

The demand curve applies to all kinds of things, not just goods for sale. It also applies to labour, for example. When the price of labour – wages – is high, the demand for workers is low. As the price falls, demand increases.

The supply curve

Just as there is a curve to show the quantity of goods or resources demanded, there is a curve that goes in the opposite direction to show how supply varies with price. When the price that something can command is low, fewer producers will want to supply it, so the quantity supplied then falls. As the price rises, so the supply will rise as more people choose to sell it.

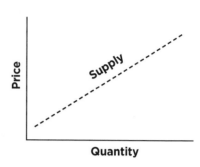

Move along

Some circumstances can cause the demand or supply curve to shift entirely to the right or left. If people have more money (incomes rise), the demand curve will probably shift to the right, but keep the same shape. The relationship between quantity and price is the same, but the absolute number of items sold increases at all points on the curve. Other changes can also affect the curve. A very hot summer might shift the curve for beer to the right (see graph); people will buy more beer at the same prices because they want it more.

If incomes decline, the curve shifts to the left, as demand falls.

The same can happen with the supply curve. If there is a bumper harvest, the supply curve for fruit will shift to the right as the price drops all along the curve. A shortage will shift the curve to the left.

Supply and demand in balance

As long as goods are available at a price that some buyers and sellers are happy with, the supply and demand curves will intersect at some point and a market will exist. Plotting the supply and demand curves on the same axes (see the graph below) shows the quantity and price where the two intersect. This will define the market for the type of goods. The same X-shaped graph can be drawn for all kinds of things that can be bought and sold.

The point where the lines cross is called the **equilibrium point** and indicates how many goods are likely to be sold and the price they are likely to fetch.

Let's suppose the graph shows the supply and demand curves for pineapples. When the price of pineapples is high, demand for them is low. As the price drops, the quantity demanded increases. When the price of pineapples is low, few producers want to supply them, so supply is low. Between the bottom ends of the supply and demand lines there is a big gap – this represents people who would like to buy pineapples at a low price, but will be frustrated as there aren't enough available.

As price rises (moving up the y-axis), more producers want to supply pineapples but fewer consumers want to buy them. At the top point on the price axis, there is another big gap. This represents the glut of pineapples that would be left unsold at this price because not enough people want to buy all those that producers would like to supply.

The sweet point

At the point of equilibrium, there are enough pineapples available to satisfy demand, at a price enough people can afford to pay, and at which suppliers can afford to produce them. If more pineapples were produced, they would remain unsold as supply would outstrip demand at this price. The shaded area in the graph on page 49

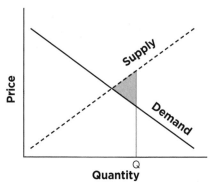

represents the pineapples that could not be sold if the quantity produced increased to Q.

Any market will naturally gravitate towards the equilibrium point unless it is prevented from doing so or is artificially altered (by a government subsidy on production, for example).

The point of equilibrium is also called the **market-clearing point**, as it is the point at which the whole quantity supplied should be sold, leaving the market clear, with no disappointed buyers and no sellers encumbered with goods they can't sell. In practice, the equilibrium is not stable; frequent changes in supply, demand and price cause it to shift.

Supply, demand and competition

Competition applies generally across economics. Competition for scarce resources affects price. It is clearly related to the supply and demand curves. If there are more workers available than jobs for them to do, the supply of workers is greater than the demand and there is competition for jobs. This (in theory) will push wages down. If there are plenty of jobs and not enough workers, the supply of

labour is too low and there is competition for workers. Wages will rise as employers compete to attract workers.

If there is a scarcity of a product that people want, such as sugar or gas, its price rises; people are competing for it and are willing to pay more than usual. If there is more of a product than people want to buy, its price goes down. The relationship can be used to manipulate markets. If governments want more people to borrow money, they reduce interest rates. The general idea is that market forces will operate: supply and demand will adjust until the right level is reached for everything.

Entering and leaving the market

The supply of an item can't usually be arbitrarily changed immediately just because people would like to buy more or fewer. Changes in demand generally lead to changes in supply, and they do this by encouraging producers to leave or enter a market. Sometimes this can happen quickly and easily, but often it can't.

When there are very few pineapples available, demand outstrips supply – that is, more people want them than can be satisfied by the number of available pineapples. This creates competition and the price of pineapples rises. In terms of the supply curve on page 49, close to the left-hand side, quantity is low (the x-axis) and price is high (the y-axis). This is good for suppliers of pineapples but not for consumers. At this point other traders will enter the market as they see an opportunity to make money by supplying pineapples to satisfy demand. The supply of pineapples now increases. But not enough people will be willing to pay a very high price for pineapples, so to sell the extra pineapples now available the price has to come down.

If lots of new suppliers enter the pineapple market, there will be oversupply. This is the right-hand side of the graph. There are now more pineapples than people want, so to get rid of them the suppliers have to drop the price considerably. If the price goes too low, some suppliers will not be able to afford to deal in pineapples any more and will leave the market. Supply then decreases, and so the price can rise again. The market finds a new equilibrium.

Moving curves

If a market reaches an equilibrium point and the price of the item then changes, the equilibrium will move along the demand curve. If the price for an item goes up, it's likely that fewer items will be sold; if the price goes down, more will probably sell.

This can happen when external circumstances have an impact on a market. For example, if the market for pineapples was at equilibrium but then a hurricane destroyed much of the crop, the supply would drop, but the price would not have changed (though it might subsequently change).

There are also seasonal changes in the supply of/demand for some goods. Raspberries are more plentiful during the summer, so they tend to be cheaper then. In winter, raspberries have to be imported. The supply is lower, the cost higher and so the price is higher. Fewer people want to pay the higher price for raspberries in the winter, so a new supply/demand equilibrium is found.

Economics and people

On paper, it's clear: if too few people want to buy pineapples, supply will adjust until the right number of pineapples is produced for them all to sell at a price that makes pineapple-farming profitable. What this ignores is the human cost: all the 'surplus' pineapple-farmers forced into poverty, possibly along a path of anxiety, depression and despair, not knowing whether to stay with pineapples or switch to growing something else – what else? – on their now unprofitable land. Farmers probably have not wilfully set out to farm pineapples in a saturated market. They will have started to farm pineapples when pineapples were in demand, or when production methods were less efficient and the market was not yet flooded, or perhaps because they were offered incentives by their government to farm pineapples. Or maybe their family had always farmed pineapples.

And even though 'labour' is a market, labour is provided by people, and people produce all the goods and services we buy. Ethical economics must take account of people as well as numbers in its application. At this point, economics becomes political. In some areas of production – such as pineapple farming – initiatives such as 'fair trade' try to protect producers in the developing world from the worst aspects of trading in often rapacious global markets.

ADAM SMITH (1723–90)

Adam Smith was a Scots philosopher and pioneer of political economy. In 1776, he published *An Inquiry into the Nature and Causes of the Wealth of Nations* (usually just called *The Wealth of Nations*), the first modern text on economics. He set out the basis of free-market economics and explained how 'rational self-interest' and competition produce wealth and prosperity in an economy. In the first account of competition in markets, he explained how he considered competition to lead to the most productive allocation of resources. If a set of raw materials, workers and investment could be used in several different ways, competition would ensure that the most profitable use of them would predominate. Smith is especially famous for citing an 'invisible hand' which works to promote the benefit of the whole of society from the self-interested actions of individuals:

'Every individual . . . intends only his own gain, and he is in this, as in many other cases, led by an invisible hand to promote an end which was no part of his intention.'

Not that simple

In theory, markets will naturally gravitate towards the equilibrium price, but in practice other factors often intervene and market forces are not sufficiently strong to overcome them. Consequently, the optimal balance of supply and demand is not always (perhaps not often) achieved.

Markets do not exist in isolation and people do not always act rationally (or in a way that economists consider 'rational'). People in the developed world can easily get by without pineapples; it's a luxury, not a staple. How many they buy will be affected by the market for alternatives – other types of fruit, for example. If all other fruit rose in price, pineapples would seem comparatively cheaper and more people would choose to buy them. But other factors could affect people's choice to buy pineapples, including:

- a health scare that suggested pineapples are contaminated with pesticides
- a popular TV chef promoting a recipe involving pineapples
- concern for the wellbeing of workers on pineapple farms
- a news story suggesting pineapples are very good for your health
- a suggestion that eating pineapples is cool.

Ironically, even a rise in the price of pineapples could increase demand if people wanted the kudos of being seen to eat an expensive and therefore 'exclusive' item.

Time matters

If demand for a product changes, the supply is likely to change to match it. But it's important for suppliers to know whether a change in demand is a long-term trend or a short-term fad or glitch. For example, if one winter is particularly wet, the demand for wellington boots might increase. Just one rainy season is not going to attract more bootmakers into the market, though; it will take much longer than that just to set up a new factory to make boots. It is more likely that those businesses that already make boots will increase production by paying overtime to existing staff and/or taking on casual workers for a short period. But if higher levels of rainfall became the norm, perhaps because of climate change, more bootmakers would be attracted into the market. The guaranteed long-term increase in sales of wellington boots would make it worthwhile for new firms to set up in business, and for existing producers to expand to meet the new demand.

Inferior goods

People generally like to buy things of a reasonable quality if they can afford to do so. When they have little money, they might be forced to buy lower quality items. These are known as **inferior goods**. An example would be cheaply made clothes available from high street discount stores. The demand curve for inferior goods doesn't follow the usual pattern of shifting to the right as income increases. When people can afford to buy goods of better quality, they do so – the market for inferior goods decreases (the curve shifts to the left) as income increases and people have the money to pay for superior alternatives.

SOCK SHOP

Sock Shop was a specialist niche retailer founded in the UK in 1983. It sold, as the name suggests, socks. It also sold tights and small items of underwear. The shops were generally small, with many set up in railway stations. Initially very successful, Sock Shop grew fast but went into liquidation in 1990, overwhelmed by debts after a series of complex factors hit sales. Among the factors the founder, Sophie Mirman, blamed for the company's failure were a very hot summer when no one wanted to buy socks or tights, and rail strikes, which closed stations and made the company's outlets inaccessible to potential buyers.

Elasticity of demand

Economists call the extent to which the supply of, or demand for, a product changes with changing prices **price elasticity**. If a good is highly elastic, any change in price will lead to a big change in demand, and any change in supply will have a large impact on price.

This is most likely to be the case with goods for which substitutes are readily available. For example, if apple juice were to go up in price, it's likely that many people would switch to other fruit juices. A price rise of 10 per cent might lead to a drop in demand of 20 per cent or more. Demand is considered to be price elastic if a percentage change in price brings about a larger percentage change in demand; it is **inelastic** if it brings about a smaller percentage change in demand.

Some goods are inelastic in the short term but elastic in the long term. This happens if making a sudden

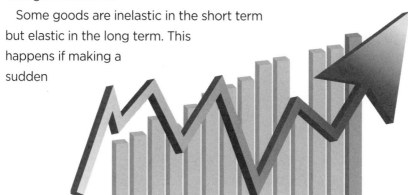

switch to another product is impractical. For example, even if oil prices were to double tomorrow, consumers would still have to fill their vehicle's petrol tank. They might cut back on non-essential journeys, but most would still have to use their cars for essential travel. So demand might fall but it would not halve. But if the change was clearly going to be long term, it would slowly lead to a permanent change in demand, as people switched to more economical vehicles, or public transport. Vehicle manufacturers would develop more fuel-efficient alternatives, such as cars powered by electricity or biofuels. In the long term, therefore, the price rise would have a more significant effect on demand – an example of price elasticity.

Lots of markets

An economy comprises many markets for many different products. All these separate markets follow the same laws of supply and demand and they are interlinked. Sometimes the link is obvious: if the supply of steel is reduced, the supply of cars made from steel will also decrease and the price of cars will go up. Some are less obviously linked. If demand for beef increases, the price of beef will go up and supply will also increase as beef producers seek to capitalize on the increased market for their product. At the same time, more leather will be produced as a by-product of the increased beef production. The supply of leather will increase, with no corresponding increase in demand, so its price will drop. If the price of foreign holidays rises, the sale of luxury goods may rise as people choose to spend their money differently.

The labour market

There is a market for labour (the work provided by employees), just as there is a market for goods and services.

In the labour market, if there is a large number of workers available, perhaps because of a rise in unemployment or an influx of cheap labour, wages will be lower. In times of high employment, when labour is scarce, employers will have to pay higher wages to attract workers.

Again, the model of the supply and demand curves is a simplification. There might be high unemployment in general, but a scarcity of workers with a particular skill, such as trained nurses. Unemployed people can't suddenly retrain to take up the vacant posts. A situation that is familiar in many industrial countries at the moment is an over supply of unskilled or semiskilled workers, but a shortage of workers with the specialist skills required. So there is a shortfall in skilled people, but a surplus of workers in general.

In some industries, there are always more people seeking work than there are jobs available for them. For example, there is never a shortage of people wanting to be footballers, actors, writers, singers or artists. Many people who would like such a job also have the necessary talents, but there are not enough jobs to go round. Consequently most people who work in these industries will be poorly paid because the oversupply means they are easily replaceable. Only the most talented (or luckiest) earn a good living from such popular jobs.

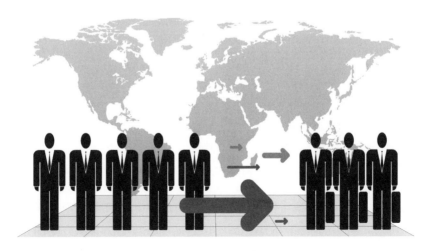

Chapter 4
Does cost reflect value?

The price label on an item in a shop only gives an indication of the cost of production.

In everyday life, the price of goods and services is generally set by the market. The value and cost of an item are related in complex ways, reflected in prices.

Buyers and sellers

If you go to a street market where you can haggle over prices, or buy items on online auction sites, you will already be used to the idea that the value of an item is fluid. It depends on what a buyer is willing to pay for an item and a seller is willing to accept for it. Generally, buyer and seller will accept a range of prices and so long as these prices coincide (or intersect) at some point a deal can be made.

In this example, the buyer and seller could make a deal at a price between

0	1	2	3	4	5	5	7
will buy							
			will sell				

$3 and $4.99. Below $3, the seller is unwilling to sell; at $5 or above, the buyer is unwilling to buy.

As this example suggests, the value of an item lies between the most and the least it can be sold for. Economists distinguish between these. The value placed on a good or service by the buyer is the most that he or she is willing to pay for it, and represents its **economic value.** At the other end of the scale, the **market value** is the lowest price at which the seller can be certain to sell.

Economic value

Economic value is a measure of the benefit or utility something provides to the buyer. This, of course, varies from one buyer to another and according to different circumstances, but the average tends to determine the price of an item. For example, suppose a small bottle of drinking water (in a  country in which the tap water is safe to drink) usually sells for $1. At a music festival on a hot day, bottled water could easily be sold for $2 a bottle as people are thirsty and have no other recourse to water. But on a cold winter day, it might be impossible to sell bottled water at all.

Neoclassical economics considers the economic value of an item to be the price it will command in a 'perfect, competitive market' – so it is equivalent to the prevailing price.

Market value

Market value is generally lower than economic value. It is the minimum for which a consumer could obtain something. For sellers, market value is the price they can expect an item to fetch. It's possible that they might be able to sell the item for less than they would like, but it must still be economic to manufacture, market and ship the item for its market value or they will not make any profit.

THE PERFECT MARKET

Economists often use the idea of a 'perfect, competitive market' in their examples, meaning a market with competition at the highest degree and no distorting factors. Other conditions are that:

- all participants have perfect knowledge of all conditions
- producers and consumers make rational decisions to maximize their self interest, which is utility for consumers and profit for producers
- producers and consumers can freely enter and leave the market at any time
- all items of output are identical and interchangeable
- all units of input, including workers, are identical and interchangeable
- there are many firms in the market
- no single firm can influence the market price, or market conditions
- there is no government regulation
- there are no external costs or benefits
- firms can only make normal profits in the long run.

This situation is never possible in reality as real markets are too varied, complex and changing.

Bread with no butter

The value of items and the market for them are rarely entirely independent of other factors. For example, if there is a bread shortage, demand for butter and other spreads – and so their market value – is likely to fall to some extent. Consumers' ability to pay for something also depends on how much money they have. For

ECONOMICS-SPEAK: MARGINAL UTILITY

The value of an item is not the same each time you buy it. The change in utility (satisfaction) that you get with each additional item of a certain type is called its **marginal utility**. If you were hungry, you would get high marginal utility from eating a sandwich. But you would get less marginal utility from eating a second sandwich. At this point you would probably not want any more. If you were then forced to have a third sandwich you did not want and which made you feel ill, you would be gaining negative marginal utility from the extra sandwich. While you might pay a lot for the first sandwich, you would not pay anything at all for the third sandwich.

example, rent and mortgage payments are bills that must be paid so if these rise people will have less money available to spend on non-essential things. The demand for, and market value of, non-essential items might then fall.

Substitute and complementary goods

The supply, demand and price curves of some goods are linked.

Substitute goods are those that can replace another good: if the price of pasta goes up, or the supply is restricted, sales of rice as a substitute good might increase.

Complementary goods are those that are bought alongside each other, so the supply, demand and price curves of one affect the sale of the other. If the supply of pasta drops, the sale of pasta sauces will fall as they are usually only used with pasta. It works the other way round, too. If the price of cinema tickets drops, the sale of popcorn in cinema foyers will rise as people go to the cinema more.

Cost of production

For a supplier, such as a manufacturer or a farmer, the value of an item can be measured in terms of what it has cost to produce. If the supplier is going to succeed in business, it's necessary to recover the **cost of production**. To make a profit, the business needs to make more from the sale of the goods than they cost to produce.

The cost of production is the total cost of the raw materials, capital used in making the goods (land, equipment and so on) and the cost of the labour, including the producer's own labour, in making and marketing the goods. Suppose someone makes bespoke rocking horses at the rate of one a week. The raw materials (wood, paint, varnish, leather, metal parts) cost $70. She pays $100 a week rent for a workshop. The cost of her equipment, averaged over its lifetime, is $20 a week (see box below). Other running costs, such as electricity, advertising and so on come to $30 a week. She doesn't employ

---

DEPRECIATING CAPITAL

Capital goods that wear out are subject to **depreciation** – the amount their value decreases (depreciates) over time. The *depreciation* of capital goods has to be taken into account by a firm as it considers the cost of producing goods. Even though the goods might last a very long time, the cost of buying, repairing, servicing and eventually replacing them must be included in the costing. Suppose it costs $1 million to equip a factory with the machinery to make plastic combs. The factory makes five million combs a year and the machinery lasts 20 years before it needs to be replaced. The cost of the machinery is spread over its lifetime so that $1 million, divided between 100 million combs (5 million x 20 years), is 1 cent per comb. That must be taken into account – along with all the other costs – when setting a price per comb.

anyone else and values her own labour at $700 a week. So she must sell each rocking horse for at least $920 (70 + 100 + 20 + 30 + 700) or she will be making a loss. In fact, she sets the price of each rocking horse at $1,100, representing

$920 costs plus $180 profit.

Value for consumers

For consumers, value is set by the benefit they hope to gain from an item. This includes taking account of **opportunity cost** (what they have given up in order to have the item). In choosing a rocking horse, consumers decide whether they (or their children) will get sufficient extra pleasure from a handmade rocking horse to justify spending $1,100 rather than buying a factory-made one from a high street store for under $100. If they bought the cheap rocking horse, they would have an extra $1,000 to spend on other things.

Many consumers won't be able to afford an expensive rocking-horse at all so the question does not arise. Some feel the beauty of the handmade item is worth the extra money, or hope to pass it on to future generations, or hope it will be an investment and rise in value. A few will be able to afford it without worrying about the money. Those who will buy at this price set the value of the utility they will gain from the rocking horse at $1,100.

Measuring utility

Some economists try to measure utility in purely financial terms. The aesthetic benefit of owning a beautiful object does not count for anything in this scheme. It gives some valuations which look odd and far from market values.

Suppose a biology student spends $75 on a textbook, but decides not to continue with biology and so never puts the knowledge he gained from the book to work. By the time he decides to get rid of it, the book has been superseded and now has no resale value ($0). He gives it away to a charity shop, which puts it on sale for $1. A teenager browsing in the shop buys the book. It inspires her to change course and study biology and she earns $50,000 more over her lifetime as a consequence. To her, the book has brought $50,000 of utility so it is very valuable. So what then is the value of the book? $0, $1, $75, or $50,000?

All that work

Another way of calculating value was first suggested by Adam Smith and adopted by Karl Marx. It calculates the value of an object in terms of the labour involved in producing it. This is called the **labour theory of value** (LTV). It tries to take account of the value of all the labour involved in the production of a good or service, including that needed to make the capital involved. In calculating the labour value of, say, hairdryers, it would be necessary to include figures for a share of making the machinery and factories involved, for designing the electronics, for running the canteen in the factory, for producing plastic from oil and so on. LTV is a feature of heterodox economics.

Use value and exchange value

Marx distinguished between **use value** and **exchange value**. Use value is a measure of how useful things are to us – the amount of utility or benefit they bring. Exchange value is the value we place on one thing in comparison to others. Typically, we think of exchange values in terms of money: we can exchange $10 for a book, for example, or for a meal in a café. This means that the book and the meal have the same exchange value.

Bubbles

Like most economic theory, the determination of use value or exchange value depends on people acting rationally in ideal market conditions. But people don't always act rationally. One result of this can be economic 'bubbles': people may pay inflated prices for goods,

'The real price of every thing, what every thing really costs to the man who wants to acquire it, is the toil and trouble of acquiring it. What every thing is really worth to the man who has acquired it, and who wants to dispose of it, or exchange it for something else, is the toil and trouble which it can save to himself, and which it can impose upon other people. That this is really the foundation of the exchangeable value of all things, excepting those which cannot be increased by human industry, is a doctrine of the utmost importance in political economy.'
Adam Smith, *The Wealth of Nations* (1776)

usually because they think they will become more valuable. When the value falls they are left with worthless belongings. The 'dotcom bubble' of the 1990s saw this phenomenon with shares in internet-based companies rocketing. Investors saw others making fortunes online so bought shares indiscriminately, including in businesses that did not have a sound business plan and had no prospect of success. As a result, these businesses were massively over-valued and quickly went bust.

One of the most bizarre and catastrophic examples of people acting irrationally in relation to value occurred in the 17th century.

Tulips were introduced to the Netherlands from Turkey in 1593 and soon became popular. Then, in the early 17th century, a virus affected the tulips that caused coloured flares to appear on the petals. The infected tulips were regarded as more attractive, so commanded a higher price. But not just a slightly higher price. As the fad for tulips flourished, so did prices. In one month, the price of tulips rose twentyfold. Convinced that prices would carry on rising, people who were not themselves tulip-traders began to invest in tulip bulbs. At the height of the craze, speculators would spend their entire life savings on tulips, or sell a house to buy a single bulb. One bulb changed hands for 5,200 florins. (It's hard to work out what a florin was worth at this point in Dutch history, but 5,200 of them was not a small amount!) When the bottom fell out of the market, the principal investors were hit very hard and some were ruined. It was the first commodity boom and crash, but certainly not the last.

During the period of so-called 'tulip mania' the use value of tulips was entirely disregarded and the exchange value became monstrously inflated. A combination of greed and panic fuelled a boom in trade that could not last, simply because the difference between use and exchange values had grown so large so quickly.

How much for those beanies?

The bubble phenomenon can even be deliberately exploited. In the 1990s, many people bought 'beanie babies' – small plush toys made by a company called Ty. Ty had a very clever marketing strategy. They persuaded people that beanie babies would become valuable, and so were an investment. Ty made many different designs, but kept each design available for only a limited time, and then 'retired' it and released a new design. In this way they engineered scarcity so that the exchange value of the toys would increase – which it did. 'Retired' beanie babies changed hands for hundreds of dollars. The exchange value of beanie babies was artificially and ridiculously high, while the use value was very low – they were essentially a $5 toy that had been hyped. There are many people today with boxes of these toys. They paid a lot of money for them, but the toys now have an exchange value that is much closer to their use value. The 'value' of beanie babies existed only in the bubble of the market.

Other measures of value

We have focused on measuring value in terms of money or exchange value, partly because there is no other universally accepted measure. Some economists have tried to measure utility value in nominal, artificial units called 'utils'. It doesn't work very well. We could say that a chair is worth 40 utils and a car is worth 5,000 utils, but the comparison is rather arbitrary. Really, if you only need a car, a chair has no use value to you at all, and vice versa.

Another way of measuring value, applicable in some circumstances, is time. We all have a finite amount of time, both in a day and in our lives. Whether we are expending our time on an activity, or simply waiting, it will have a cost in time. For example, would you prefer to pay more to have something delivered to your home rather than go to a shop to buy it? Would you be prepared to wait in a long queue simply in order to buy something more cheaply? Alternatively, would you spend more on an item you could buy locally because you value your time more than the sum of money you would save if you travelled further to get it?

As we have seen, scarcity can bestow value and can even be manipulated to make things with low intrinsic or utility value and little lasting exchange value seem valuable. A piece of art seems a safe investment. Surely works by a great – but deceased – artist will always keep their worth, as these are in short supply and each one

is unique? Yet, fashions and tastes in art change, and the work of an artist who has fallen out of favour – or whose name has been linked with scandal – may fall in value, even though the pictures themselves remain unchanged.

Chapter 5

How do we know if a country is rich or poor?

Do you live in a rich country? You probably know roughly, but measuring the comparative wealth of countries is a tricky process.

If someone asked you how much money you have, you might think of the cash in your pocket or the total money deposited in your bank account. You might also include the value of your possessions, or at least the big ones, such as a house and a car. If you own stocks and shares, those are also part of your wealth. Another way of thinking of your wealth is in terms of income. Similarly, when we talk about wealthy nations, we can take account of the country's reserves – the stock of money, gold and other assets it has – and its income. In general, income is more important.

Wealth of nations

There is a strong correlation between wealth and income, more so in the case of nations than with individuals. Individuals might be wealthy but have little income if, for instance, they have inherited property or saved money and don't work. Economists consider wealth to be a stock of assets that produce income. On the whole, nations are less likely than individuals to leave valuable assets languishing – they are most likely to put them to work to generate income. It is reasonable, then, that the wealth of nations is usually compared by estimating their levels of income.

The income of a country is often reported in terms of **Gross Domestic Product**, or GDP. There are other ways of measuring income, but this is the most widely used. GDP is a measure of the value of everything that a nation produces. It works from the final value of goods and services (that is, everything produced), so it includes taxes on spending, such as **value added tax** (VAT).

Calculating GDP

The figures for GDP are calculated from millions of tax returns and other documents collected by governments. They are never fully accurate; some people make mistakes in returns, some don't complete them honestly (or at all).

There are also some types of 'product' that are not bought and sold. In the UK, for instance, healthcare is funded by the government – the patient pays nothing other than a charge for prescribed medicines from a pharmacy. Only 10 per cent of prescriptions attract even that charge. Medicines, surgical procedures and care in hospital are 'free at the point of use' for UK nationals.

This means that most of the output of the National Health Service (NHS) would not show up in GDP unless there was another way of accounting for it. The solution is to include the cost to the government of providing healthcare. For the year 2015–16, the budget for the NHS was assessed at £115.4 billion (around $180 billion). This figure is included in GDP as income (the value of services produced) from the NHS.

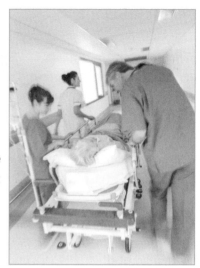

How better can be worse

One oddity resulting from accounting for productivity by looking at cost is that if a service becomes more efficient, costing less to deliver the same service, it looks as though less has been produced. Suppose nurses take on some tasks previously carried out by doctors; nurses are paid less than doctors, so the cost of providing treatment falls, but the same number of patients are being treated. An improvement in efficiency (a good thing) looks like a fall in productivity (a bad thing) with this form of accounting.

What's missing?

GDP can only cover goods and services that are declared. That means that the hidden (or 'black') economy does not feature in GDP, nor do goods and services for which no money changes hands.

The hidden economy covers the informal exchanges that seek to avoid taxation through undeclared cash transactions. If a householder pays cash to a gardener to mow the lawn, or to a bricklayer to construct a wall, there may be no official paper trail of the work or the payment. Self-employed workers who are paid in cash might choose to declare only part (or even none) of their income to the tax authorities. In this way, they avoid paying taxes. This is, of course, illegal but also difficult to monitor. Electronic bank transfers and cheque payments leave a trace that the tax authorities can find, but cash does not. There are other reasons for not declaring income. Someone may wish to continue claiming welfare benefits that would be removed if the claimant's true income was known (also illegal), or because the income is from an illegal activity such as drug dealing that they can't declare or they would be prosecuted.

Doing it for yourself

Not everything missing from GDP is illegal or fraudulent. A lot of work produces no accountable income, but does generate value. Anyone who undertakes a do-it-yourself (DIY) home refurbishment project or grows their own fruit and vegetables has generated a valuable product that they might otherwise have paid for. Childcare, looking after older relatives, and household chores are all services that can be paid for but which are often provided for free within families. In some parts of

the world, people engage in subsistence farming, meaning that they grow food solely for their own families to eat rather than for sale to the public. This does not appear in the GDP of the country, but is a very important source of value for the population.

Uses of GDP

Economists use GDP as a measure of the standard of living in a country. By comparing the GDP currently and in previous years, they can gain an idea of how the standard of living has either improved or deteriorated. By comparing the GDP of different countries, they can rank them in order of prosperity and living standards.

Comparing GDP over time

Although, as we have seen, there are some things that are not accounted for in GDP, these do not greatly matter if we are using GDP to compare the changing wealth of a country over time. The relative values of the hidden economy and of home-produced services such as childcare and DIY are likely to be roughly the same, at least over short periods of time.

If the GDP of a nation increases over time, this suggests that living standards are improving. It's not quite that straightforward, though. **Inflation** also has to be taken into account (see page 173). Inflation is a sustained rise in general prices over time. This means that over a period of inflation the same sum of money is exchanged for less in terms of goods and services. If the GDP of a nation rose from $200 billion to $210 billion over a period of five years (a rise of 5 per cent) but prices rose 10 per cent over that period, the standard of living would actually have fallen – the $210 billion would represent less in terms of goods and services than the original $200 billion. To avoid inflation skewing the results of a comparison, economists distinguish between **nominal GDP** and **real GDP**. Nominal GDP is the calculated figure, not taking account of prices. Real GDP is corrected to take account of the retail price index and so is more useful for comparative purposes.

Another factor not shown by GDP is the size of the population. If the GDP of a nation increases by 5 per cent over a period, but the population increases by 10 per cent, there will have been a fall in average living standards as each person will have a smaller share of GDP. We can take account of this by calculating and comparing **per capita GDP** – that is, the GDP divided by the population.

Still not right

There are still some problems that calculating real, per capita GDP does not address.

Just as increased efficiency can look like a drop in productivity, so can an increase in quality, if it comes at no extra cost. The true cost of electronic goods has fallen over the last few decades while their speed, quality and storage capabilities have increased many times. The sale of a computer in 2015 for $500 shows up in GDP as less valuable than the sale of a computer for $1,000 in 1990, yet the computer sold in 2015 will be much more powerful than the earlier model. Conversely, scarcity can raise prices. If the price of oil doubles and consumption falls by a quarter, spending on oil has increased; this means that GDP increases, but productivity and standards of living fall.

Rising GDP apparently suggests a rising standard of living, but this is not always the case. Increases in public spending add to GDP, but, in reality, some might mean a fall in the standard of living. During wartime, spending on defence is very high. This shows up in the country's accounts as a rise in GDP, but people might be enduring a much lower standard of living than in peacetime. Similarly, civil unrest or high crime rates might lead to increased spending on policing, again raising GDP – yet people have a lower standard of living when surrounded by riots, crime and falling bombs.

Even very high GDP might not reflect a good standard of living for most people if there is great inequality in a country. Rising GDP can be accounted for by a small wealthy class spending extravagantly while the majority of people have a falling standard of living (see page 184 – *If we are the 99 per cent, who are the 1 per cent?*).

Splurging

If you took out all your savings and bought new furniture and clothes, ate in expensive restaurants and took foreign holidays, you would enjoy a high standard of living now, but the future would be rather bleak unless you could easily replace the money. It's the same for a nation. Nations need to balance investment and consumption. If a nation spends all its money in the short term and doesn't invest, GDP will rise immediately, but in all likelihood will be lower later on. In democratic countries, governments are elected to serve for a limited term. The temptation to 'spend now and pay later', thereby attracting support from voters, can be considerable. It means the financial consequences of a spending programme might not be felt until the next government is in power.

> **CHANGING GDP**
>
> A simple equation allows economists to work out how long it will take to double or halve GDP, given a rate of change.
>
> If the rate of increase is g per cent, it will take 70/g years to double.
>
> So if the rate of increase was 3.5 per cent, it would take 70 ÷ 3.5 = 20 years for GDP to double.
>
> If the rate of change was 2 per cent, it would take 70 ÷ 2 = 35 years for GDP to double.

Mine is bigger than yours

GDP is often used as a way of comparing the standard of living or wealth of two or more nations. Again, it's important to take account of the number of people to calculate per capita GDP. Otherwise, if we worked just with total GDP, a country with a small wealthy population could look worse off than a country with a very large, but poor, population.

Whose currency?

One difficulty with comparing national economies is deciding which currency to use. If the GDP of the UK is reported in pounds sterling (£), that of Eurozone countries in euros (€) and of the USA in dollars ($), how can they be compared? The exchange rate fluctuates and if one currency is particularly strong (or weak) on the day the comparison is made, that might give a distorted picture of the relative wealth of the countries.

Instead, it's common to use international dollars, (Int$), sometimes also called the Geary–Khamis dollar, named after Roy Geary and Salem Hanna Khamis, the economists who proposed and developed the idea. The international dollar is equivalent in terms of purchasing power to the US$ at a specified moment in time, often 1999 or 2000.

Here are some figures for national GDP for the year 2014, taken from the International Monetary Fund's data:

Country	Per capita GDP, Int $	Ranking
Qatar	143,427	1
Luxembourg	92,049	2
Norway	66,937	6
USA	54,597	10
Australia	46,433	15
Germany	45,888	18
Canada	44,843	20
France	40,375	24
UK	39,511	27
Japan	37,390	28
New Zealand	35,152	31
Russia	24,805	49
Mexico	17,881	66
South Africa	13,046	87
India	5,855	125
Bangladesh	3,373	142
Niger	1,048	182
Central African Republic	607	187

The per capita GDP of the whole world was Int$15,147 in April 2015.

DIY disruption

Cultural patterns vary between nations and this can affect GDP in
a way that makes meaningful comparison difficult. Domestically

produced goods – DIY, growing vegetables, looking after children, for example – can be particularly disruptive in comparing the GDP of different nations.

If we look at the per capita GDP of some economies, it looks as though they should not be sustainable. How can the Central African Republic survive if production is Int$607 per year (less than Int$2 a day) per person? This is because many people produce food and other goods that they make and grow for themselves, which don't show up in the formal economy and therefore do not appear in GDP. If a farmer hatches chicks from her hens and raises more chickens for meat and eggs, which she either eats or barters with neighbours for other goods, this productivity is not recognized in the international financial markets. Yet the amount a person in the USA spends on eggs and chicken – and other items the African farmer has bartered for – might represent several hundred dollars of GDP. It could be more than the entire per capita GDP of the Central African Republic.

Even growing lots of vegetables, building your own house and keeping chickens, it would be pretty hard to survive in the USA on the average income of a resident of the Central African Republic. This is because things cost a lot more in the USA, and there are more necessary expenses, such as heating, lighting and transport. So the relative costs of items in different countries are compared using **purchasing power parity**.

ECONOMICS-SPEAK: PURCHASING POWER PARITY

Purchasing power parity is a way of comparing the purchasing power (what can be bought for each unit of currency) of two different national currencies. It is calculated by comparing the prices of two identical items with the official exchange rate of the currencies. For example, if the exchange rate of Chinese yuan to euros is 7:1, for the two currencies to have equal purchasing power, an item that costs 1 euro in Spain should cost 7 yuan in China. If the item costs 4 yuan, someone in China could buy more with the same amount of money, so the purchasing power of the yuan would be higher than that of the euro.

Buying what's needed

The items individuals need to pay for vary with circumstances, too. Scandinavians pay a lot for heating fuel, but in Niger this level of expenditure is not necessary because the climate is much warmer. In the USA, most people have to pay for transport to get to work, but in some poorer economies most people simply walk to work. In the USA, most people pay for healthcare through health insurance, but in the UK healthcare is provided by central government and paid for through taxation. All these differences affect standards of living and comparisons between countries. If you don't need to buy as much, you don't need to earn as much.

Chapter 6

How did we get here?

Modern economics systems have developed over a very long period of time, during which they have adapted as societies have changed.

You are almost certainly reading this book in a country with a well-established economy and one that has at least some elements of **capitalism**. Capitalism is an economic system based on the principle that business is run to make a profit. It's the dominant economic system in the world today. But how did we get it? (There is more about the nature, advantages and disadvantages of capitalism on page 102 – *Is the whole world capitalist now?*).

The capitalist marketplace

Capitalism posits three markets: the market for labour (people working for money); the market for goods and services (things you can buy); and the financial market (buying and selling intangible products related to money). It might seem that we could get along quite well with only the first two. No one would need to make a profit – they would just need to earn enough to buy the things they needed and that would be fine.

This type of system has been common in the past and still exists in some parts of the world. Each person produces things that he or she sells or trades for other things that they need. Before that, each person grew or made all the things they needed. It's subsistence living, generally seen in subsistence farming when each family produces what they consume in terms of food and materials. (This type of economy is also called an **autarky**.) It doesn't work very well. We would each need, say, a few chickens, part ownership of a cow, some land to grow wheat and vegetables, timber and tools to make furniture (and how did you mine and smelt the iron to make the tools?).

Economy starter-kit

If you want to build an economy, you need to separate tasks and people doing them – that gives potential for growth. And growth means – or should mean – that everyone can have a better lifestyle.

Specialization of labour made sense early on. One person gets really good at making woollen capes from the wool another person's sheep produce. Someone else grows lots of vegetables. In total, the society can produce more than if everyone is struggling to supply all their own needs inefficiently, doing some tasks they are not very

good at as well as those they can do well. Money became useful at this point – an economy based on tokens is easier to manage than if everyone barters directly (see page 20 – *What is money anyway?*).

If it all goes well, society has a surplus of goods and can trade with other societies. As people travel further afield, they find new markets and new products. When

Europeans discovered South America they found tobacco, chocolate, potatoes and tomatoes which they introduced to Europe and which became items of international trade. North American Indians found they could trade a useless tract of land such as Manhattan Island for a handful of shiny beads they wanted; the beads were not valued very highly in Europe. Everyone was – briefly – happy.

Growing the economy

That's all very well for starters, but a simple mercantile exchange economy like this can't progress very far – and it means the society itself can't make much progress. While everyone is making or growing things for immediate sale or consumption, there is no capacity for research and development. Who is going to have the time to design a steam engine? Who is going to have the money to build a rail network?

Capitalism allows larger-scale, longer-term projects. Research and development, and expansion in manufacturing or service enterprises all need investment. This involves being less economically productive in the short term, while developing products or doing research in order to be more economically productive in the long run. Unless someone can save the money an enterprise needs for such a venture, they must borrow it. And why would anyone lend the money – which they could lose if it all goes wrong – unless they stand to

gain something? So a system
developed in which investors
would lend their money to
businesses in the hope of getting
more back in return. To pay them
back, the businesses need to
make a profit. And so at a stroke
we have the three markets:
labour, goods and services, and
finance. That's a great over-

simplification, of course. But you get the general idea. The problem
has not gone away with passing time. In developing economies
today, there are many small-scale entrepreneurs and self-employed
people, but they can't develop their businesses without capital.

Again and again: division of labour

One of the ways in which production can be made more efficient is
by the division of labour. A single individual carrying out a complex,
multistage task is not as productive as a group of people each
undertaking part of the task and doing that same part repeatedly.
This can only happen when someone takes an overview of a process
and decides to increase productivity by splitting the task into more
efficient units. The process then needs organizing so that part-made

products are passed on at an efficient rate: it would be inefficient if one person took just a minute to complete a task, but was held up through waiting for someone else whose task took five minutes. If the division has to be unequal, more people need to be employed on the slow tasks than on the quick tasks to improve production flow.

Once tasks have been broken down into discrete units in this way, they often become easier to mechanize. Many factory jobs that involve simple tasks such as assembling or welding components have been taken over by machinery.

PIN MONEY

Economist Adam Smith used the example of manufacturing pins to show how the division of labour can make a business profitable. Far beyond the separation of growing, processing and weaving wool between different tradespeople, Smith suggested that a simple procedure such as making pins from wire could be broken into stages, and each stage carried out by a different worker. He claimed that whereas a worker making pins from start to finish could complete 20 pins a day, ten workers each specializing in one or two stages could, between them, make 48,000 pins a day. In 1832, pin factories were producing 8,000 pins a day per worker (nearly double the 1776 rate), and in 1980, with considerable mechanization, they made 800,000 pins a day per worker.

From feudalism to merchants

The economic system in medieval Europe was known as feudalism. Serfs, or peasants – the poorest people in society – worked land that was owned by their local lord (hence the term 'landlord'). In exchange for their labour, serfs were given certain meagre benefits, such as food, shelter and protection from other lords. There was no competition, no free market and serfs had little or no choice in who they worked for. Wealth was retained by the lords and was largely inherited (or seized in battle). It did not transfer to the serfs, no matter how hard they worked. It was hardly an equitable state of affairs.

By the Renaissance period, feudalism had given way to a mercantile style of economy, with the emergence of banks (first in Italy) and the growth of international trade. Individuals had more freedom; they were

THE BLACK DEATH: DEATH TO FEUDALISM?

Some economic historians claim that feudalism was ended by the Black Death, a pandemic that killed up to a third of the population of Europe and Asia in the 1340s. The plague killed so many labourers that huge tracts of land lay deserted, the crops rotting in the fields and nothing being planted. Once the plague passed, the surviving labourers were able to demand much better conditions in exchange for their work. Following the law of supply and demand, the supply of labourers had fallen and demand was high, so those still in the market were able to secure better terms. These terms included freedom of movement, the freedom to work for a master of their choice, and better remuneration.

no longer serfs and – at least in theory – had more choice over where they worked, for how much and at what type of job. Merchants ruled the system, and made most of their money by trading goods – buying them cheaply in one market and selling them at a profit in another. Mercantilism encouraged minimal imports and maximum exports with the aim of acquiring bullion (gold and silver) from other nations. The idea rested on the principle of a fixed sum in the world economy, and one country could only gain money at the expense of another country. To protect home markets, governments introduced import controls, subsidies for home-produced goods and protectionist tariffs (charges imposed on imports to protect the home market). Modern economies also adopt this strategy sometimes; both the USA and Japan limit imports in this way.

We can all get richer

From the 18th century, economic theorists such as David Hume and Adam Smith challenged the idea that the total wealth of the world was fixed and in the 19th century Britain abandoned its protectionist system of tariffs.

The Industrial Revolution brought proper capitalism

[The prevention of poverty requires the] 'opening and well-balancing of trade; the cherishing of manufacturers; the banishing of idleness; the repressing of waste and excess by sumptuary laws; the improvement and husbanding of the soil; [and] the regulation of prices.'
Francis Bacon, *Of Seditions and Troubles* (1625)

HOW TO GET RICHER

It might seem counterintuitive that we can all get richer without someone else getting poorer, but it's possible if productivity increases. By adopting more efficient systems of production, we can produce more from the same inputs, and that generates prosperity. It works even at a personal level. If you have $5 and buy a fish to cook, you have one meal. If you spend it on a fishing rod, you might catch lots of fish dinners. Similarly, you could spend the money on a bag of apples or an apple tree sapling and get years of apple crops.

with it – archetypal, top-hatted, capitalist factory owners who 'ground the faces of the workers into the dirt' (pretty much literally). In the early years, with no legislation to protect workers, abuses were rampant. The western nations – at least some of them – still had child

labour; it was definitely not a good time and place to be at the bottom of the hierarchy. The 'dark Satanic mills' of England mentioned by William Blake in his poem 'And did those feet in ancient time' (1808) belong to this period. From the late 19th century, legislation was introduced to give more protection to the vulnerable.

Chapter 7

Is the whole world capitalist now?

It's rarely the case that a nation has the chance to design its economy from the ground up.

The major economies have developed naturally over time. When America formed its own constitution, it brought from Europe many ideas about statecraft and economics that became enshrined in the new nation state and a **free market economy** was one of them.

Free-market and command economies

A free-market economy operates in the ways we have seen so far: individuals and firms own capital and they use it in combination with labour, land and its resources, to produce goods and services for sale. These are sold on the open market for whatever price they can command, following the rules of supply and demand. The market – the willingness of people to buy and sell – determines what will be produced, for whom, and how.

The opposite of a free-market economy is a **command economy**. In this, the government or the state owns the capital and decides what will be produced, how it will be produced, how much it will be sold for and who it will be sold to. Command economies are associated with communist countries such as the former USSR, Cuba, China and North Korea.

The principal distinction between free and command economies is ownership of the means of production. In a free-market economy, the means of production are held by individuals and firms (which are themselves owned by individuals, either in their entirety or through shareholdings). In a command economy, the government owns the means of production on behalf of the people.

All's fair – or not

In an ideal world, a command economy benignly run should produce a fair and equitable state. In the real world, this doesn't happen. There is always a concentration of wealth, through corruption and self-interest, that appears with the emerging ruling class. At the bottom end of the scale, workers might suffer shortages

and have little choice over what they can buy, what to do with their time and how they live.

When the government controls production, and there is no competition between producers, there is no incentive to provide a wide choice of goods. Indeed, producing a wide choice of goods is economically foolhardy as effort is duplicated and production less efficient. Why run two factories producing different styles of car when you could run one slightly larger factory producing only one style of car? Without private owners who are keen to make a profit from selling their model, there is no incentive to

improve the single model of car to attract more customers.

Lack of competition leads to poor standards and uniformity. This is what happened in the communist command economies of Eastern Europe in the years after World War II. As the people saw the variety and quality of goods in western markets, they became increasingly dissatisfied with what their own command economy could provide. More wanted to leave to seek a better standard of living, and the communist regimes had to police their borders to prevent mass defection to the West.

On the positive side, a command economy can (if properly run) make high standards of healthcare and education available to all. The processes in the USSR for identifying children with talent in sport and music, for instance, and tutoring them intensively at no cost to their parents, led to some triumphs of achievement. (Again, lack of choice has its downside – we don't know how many chosen children were coached and then rejected, or coached when they would rather not have been, causing psychological and emotional damage.)

One and all

A command economy has little space for individuality. A person with a bright idea, particular talent or entrepreneurial spirit can't put it to use to increase their personal wealth – it can only be used for the benefit of society as a whole. That is not necessarily a bad thing, and different societies have different ways of evaluating and appreciating the link

between the individual and society. Scientists and artists in the USSR achieved feats every bit as great as their counterparts in free-market economies, but even there competition (this time with the West) spurred them on. This can quickly lead us into areas of psychology and sociology which, while relevant to economics, are outside the scope of this book. The evidence of the command economies of the 20th century, though, suggests that without the enticement of personal gain or recognition, some aspects of economic activity fall behind because people lack the motivation to improve.

The focus on equality in the communist states of the 20th century was not a direct result of the economic system, but had a detrimental impact on it. Instead of putting labour to its best use, some regimes launched an assault on intellectuals by, for example, forcing them to work on collective farms or in factories. In China and Cambodia, in particular, the war against the elite led to considerable human capital being wasted, not to mention extreme personal suffering. The result was that countries with immense natural resources and populations ended up with much lower productivity, and consequently a much lower standard of living for most people, than could have been achieved in a free-market economy.

The other side of the fence

On the other hand, a free-market economy has its own problems. The means of production can easily become concentrated in the hands of a few, who become an elite and protect their positions and possessions aggressively.

A free-market economy allows the market to decide what is made and sold, for what prices, and to whom. The market decides, also, who benefits from production. As consumers have free choice between goods of many types, they dictate what is sold: they won't buy things they don't want and they won't buy at prices they can't afford. In theory, competition between suppliers will drive prices down to an equilibrium point, and at the same time it will ensure plenty of choice. In fact, it falls short of this ideal.

In the case of essential goods – housing, food, heating and water, for instance – people are forced to pay the price set by the market whether they like it or not. There is little or no competition in some energy markets, for example. A market with only one supplier is called a monopoly. It's impossible for

ECONOMICS-SPEAK: MONOPOLIES AND OLIGOPOLIES

A **monopoly** is the market condition that is directly opposite to competition. In a monopoly there is only one supplier or producer in the market and there are barriers to entry that prevent others starting up. These barriers might be financial, legal or physical. For example, the Saudi government controls the rights to extracting and selling oil in Saudi Arabia, so no other company can start up.

An **oligopoly** exists when just a few suppliers or producers control a market. The oligopoly effectively controls prices; if one supplier drops their prices the others will follow suit to avoid losing their portion of the customers (**market share**).

a new water company, for example, to enter the market in a country where mains water and sewerage are already established and privately owned. They would need to reach some agreement with the company supplying the infrastructure.

Mixed economies

In practice, most economies today are mixed economies. They have a free market for luxury goods while some essential goods and services are produced for the benefit of everyone, using public money. These might include any or all of: the supply of amenities, such as water, electricity, and gas; healthcare services including hospitals, family doctors and dentists; and transport, such as railways, bus networks and a national airline.

Some goods and services have to be provided by the state, even in a free-market economy. Examples are roads, the police force and the army. It is not possible to exclude some people from the benefits of protection by the police or the army, so this is available to everyone, whether or not they pay anything towards them (see page 165).

The extent of the free market in a mixed economy varies. Healthcare and education are examples of services that can be supplied freely to all citizens, or can be charged for. In some countries (such as the UK and USA), there are both public and private versions available and people can choose whether to use the free public service or pay for a private service that might (or might not) be better. The USA has more of a free-market approach to healthcare than the UK, with those who can afford it paying for private healthcare insurance and those who can't falling back on state provision. In the UK, the National Health Service promises good quality healthcare to all citizens, paid for entirely through taxation and 'free at the point of delivery'. The UK also has private healthcare provision, sometimes chosen by people who want and can afford an alternative to the state system.

We can measure how mixed or free a market is by looking at the proportion of GDP that goes on government spending. Overall, the UK has a more free-market approach than some other EU countries. The graph opposite shows that Germany and the UK, up to 2012, had more mixed economies than the USA. The USA is the largest free-market economy in the world. It has a low level of welfare support and public provision and high levels of social inequality (see page 185). The Scandinavian countries spend a higher proportion of their national income on public goods and provide such benefits as free

Public spending as a share of GDP in selected countries

Between 1980 and 2018 (%)

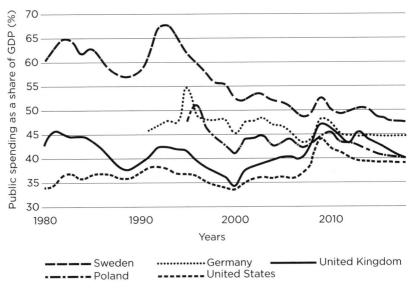

The earliest data for Poland comes from 1995; data since 2012 are IMF projections
Source: own study on basis of IMF data.

childcare and a higher level of environmental protection. People in Scandinavia have, on average, a higher standard of living than people elsewhere and a lower level of social inequality. All this provision comes at the expense of far higher taxes (see page 122), leaving consumers with less choice of how to spend their money as they have less left over to spend as they wish.

Flavours of capitalism

Capitalism is not all one flavour, as we have seen. **Laissez-faire** or liberal capitalism believes in leaving as much as possible to market forces, with minimal legislation or government intervention. In the UK, this approach was favoured by the Victorian industrialists and led to extreme poverty and social inequality. Today, it is seen in many developing countries where it leads to sweatshops, child and slave labour, and terrible working conditions.

The British economist John Maynard Keynes (1883–1946) advocated a degree of government intervention in the market – even in a free-market society – to ensure the market operates at an optimum level. This has become known as **Keynesian capitalism**. Western industrialized nations with mixed economies try to achieve a balance between intervention and market forces. Where exactly the right balance lies is debated by economists and is a main bone of contention between politicians on the right and left.

Those on the right favour reducing government intervention as much as possible and maximizing competition, choice and market forces on the grounds that this leads to a stronger economy which provides increased opportunities for everyone. Those on the left favour public ownership of key industries, an enlarged welfare state and increased legislation to protect consumers, workers and the disadvantaged on the grounds that a totally free market is inherently

biased in favour of the employers at the expense of the workers. Most western politicians generally try to find a middle way between these two extremes.

Chapter 8

Why do we pay taxes?

'Tis impossible to be sure of any thing but Death and Taxes.' Christopher Bullock (1716)

People grumble about taxes, and some expend considerable effort to avoid paying them. Yet taxes are essential if we want the government to provide public goods and services – the things that everyone needs, from a police force to roads and schools.

ECONOMICS-SPEAK: DIRECT AND INDIRECT TAXATION

Economists divide taxes into **direct** and **indirect**.

A direct tax is taken from the tax-payer when money is earned, and it is paid straight to the government's collecting agency. Examples include income tax, collected from individuals, and corporation tax, based on the profits of businesses.

An indirect tax is collected by an intermediary, such as a retailer, at the point of sale, and passed on to the government's collecting agency later. Examples are sales tax or value added tax (VAT), usually applied as a flat percentage rate to all products, and specific excise taxes on alcohol and petrol, which vary between products.

Most economies have a mix of taxes, some of which are direct and some indirect. There is generally some level of taxation on income: on wages (for individuals) and profit (for businesses). This can be a flat rate, fixed at one level, or progressive, with the level of taxation rising as income rises. There may be both a national and local tax on goods and services, as in the USA. Essential items might be exempt or taxed at a lower rate. In the UK, for example, VAT is not charged on most foods, children's clothes and books.

Types of tax

Some transfers of goods or money attract additional taxes. Buying or selling land or real estate, for example, might attract so-called stamp duty. Originally this was a charge for having the documentation of the transfer authorized – or 'stamped'. The stamp itself has gone, but the duty remains. Taxes involving the transfer of wealth are often set at a much higher rate. These include **inheritance tax** – tax on money, goods and property passed on following death – and **capital gains tax** – levied on the sale of high-value items, including land and real estate.

In some countries, there is a tax on valuable goods owned by individuals, such as large houses or works of art.

Tourist taxes are a way of charging for the strain put on infrastructure by a large number of visitors. Venice is an example of a city that imposes an overnight tax on visitors.

Controlling behaviour with taxes

Excise duties are taxes on the manufacture or distribution of certain types of goods. They can include import duties on goods brought in from abroad. Excise duties on luxury goods or items such as tobacco, alcohol and sugary drinks (informally known as 'sin taxes') that are

WHAT CAN YOU TAX?

Some pretty strange things have been taxed in the past, with governments either trying to dissuade people from certain behaviours or profit from them.

In Ancient Rome, freedom was taxed for slaves who had earned enough to buy themselves out of slavery, as was urine (when sold for use in tanneries and other industries). In medieval Europe, there was a tax on soap.

Britain in particular has produced some pretty unusual taxes. Over the course of the 18th century, it taxed windows (if the house had more than ten), fireplaces, bricks, wig powder, candles and printed wallpaper. All these taxes were specifically targeted at the rich. You can still see bricked up windows in some English country houses of the period, a result of trying to reduce the tax burden on the house. People tried to avoid brick taxes by using fewer larger bricks (though these too were soon taxed at a higher rate). To avoid tax on printed wallpaper they hung plain wallpaper and then painted designs onto it.

regarded as unhealthy can be used as a form of social engineering – by making consumption expensive, a government can discourage it.

The opposite of using taxes as a disincentive is to remove taxes to encourage (or 'incentivize') a particular form of behaviour. For example, a government might make sports equipment or healthy foods exempt from sales tax.

These taxes and exemptions to influence people's behaviour are not entirely altruistic – a healthy population is more economically productive than an unhealthy population, and requires less spending on healthcare and welfare.

Not a tax but a charge

Some things that look like taxes are not, in economists' terms, taxes at all. In the UK, people in work pay tax on their income and also National Insurance (NI) contributions. Although NI looks like a tax (it is a percentage of income above a certain level of earnings, taken by the government) it is technically regarded as a charge for the services provided by the welfare state. These include free healthcare, welfare benefits for people who are unemployed or on low incomes, and pensions for the elderly. Compulsory payments to a local authority or utility (such as Council Tax in the UK) pay for local services such as education, refuse collection, police, and road maintenance.

Shifting the tax burden

How and how much individuals and businesses are taxed is decided by a state's government. It often changes with a change of government and can also be changed during times of crisis, such as war – an expensive undertaking that needs considerable funds.

The way the tax burden is allocated reflects the values of a society or its government and the type of economic model it favours.

A left-leaning government in a mixed economy will generally impose higher taxes (especially on the rich) so that more can be provided in terms of state provision (such as infrastructure and welfare). The left-wing approach favours supporting the less fortunate so that they have an acceptable standard of living, and reducing inequality. This is funded by a high level of direct taxation and sometimes higher indirect taxes on non-essential or luxury items.

A right-leaning government will tend to reduce taxes and, correspondingly, reduce public spending. The right-wing approach favours encouraging businesses and individuals to strive by rewarding effort and profitability with high, minimally taxed income, aiming to improve prosperity overall. It is common for right-wing governments to charge a low level of direct taxes and a high level of indirect taxes. Indirect taxes (typically taxes on spending) are within

WHAT'S ESSENTIAL?

In setting indirect taxation on non-essential goods, economists and politicians have to decide which goods are essential. It leads to some odd distinctions within categories. In the UK most food items are regarded as essential and attract no VAT. However, there is VAT on hot food, crisps, roasted, salted nuts (but not unsalted, raw nuts), biscuits (but not cakes), fruit juice (but not fruit). There is no VAT on meat, as long as it is a species usually considered to be food – so VAT is charged on crocodile, ostrich and horse meat. There is no VAT on 'normal' vegetables but there is on, for example, ornamental cabbages. There is no VAT on live fish of species usually eaten but there is VAT on ornamental fish, unless they are prepared for consumption. There is VAT on animal food only if the animal is not of a type usually eaten in Britain – so there is VAT on dog food, but not on chicken feed.

Children's clothes and shoes attract no VAT. There is no VAT on a towel with a hood that can be wrapped around a baby, but there is VAT on a towel with no hood. A hat made with real fur on the outside attracts VAT, unless it is sheepskin or rabbit fur, but a hat made with artificial fur or with fur only on the inside attracts no VAT. There is no VAT on a child's scarf, but there is on scrunchies and earmuffs. There is no VAT on dressing-up outfits, including accessories such as toy guns and handcuffs, as long as they are sold as part of an entire outfit.

people's control as they can choose to spend or not spend their money on items that attract taxation.

Indirect taxation on purchases has the advantage for a government or local authority that it is not limited to residents, but must also be paid by visitors and tourists who would not otherwise contribute to a country's taxation.

What's it for?

The income from taxes is spent on many essential things:

- running the process of government itself and the state in general
- enforcing law and order (policing) and national security (military)
- maintaining infrastructure (roads, canals, data cabling, public transport, etc.).

And, to varying degrees:

- funding healthcare, education and a welfare state
- running state-owned services providing utilities such as gas, electricity and water
- providing sports facilities, museums and libraries, and supporting the arts.

The income from some types of tax can be earmarked for specific services. For instance, a tax on road use could be set aside to fund road-building or public transport. This is known as ring-fencing or **hypothecation**. It is often appropriated for other uses, however.

Against taxes

Those who favour a free-market economy are often opposed to taxation as it reduces people's choice of how to spend their money. They consider that taxation distorts the market. This is because the way taxes are spent is decided by the government and might not reflect an individual's preferences. For example, childless citizens would not normally spend money on children's education, but have no choice when this is funded from the taxation that everyone must pay. One extreme view is that taxation represents coercion or theft as people have no choice about whether to pay it and so 'buy' the services the government has chosen.

Setting the rate

Governments have to find a balance when setting taxes. Tax rates have to be set at a level that will raise enough money to fund their spending programme. But if tax rates are too high it acts as a disincentive to work and so reduces the amount of tax revenue collected. Some economists maintain that if tax rates are kept low, people have an incentive to work more because they get to keep more of the income they earn. When they spend or invest that money, it makes the economy more vigorous, leading to more revenue in taxes later. There might even be an increase immediately as people will work longer hours and so pay more tax overall, even though it is at a lower rate. If tax rates are higher, people see little 'marginal benefit' (increased income per hour or day worked) and so might choose to work less, causing tax revenues to drop. Some of the very rich might move abroad, to countries with lower tax rates, if they believe the tax burden is too great.

The Laffer Curve (below) shows how the relationship between taxation rate and revenue works. The peak of the curve indicates the rate where most tax is collected. Its shape is disputed, however, and probably varies by time and place. It might be symmetrical, with most tax collected at a tax rate of 50 per cent or less, or it might be asymmetrical. There might even be two peaks. The idea of the curve goes back to 14th-century Tunisia and the Arab proto-sociologist Ibn Khaldun, though it is named after American economist Arthur Laffer (who made no claim to have invented it).

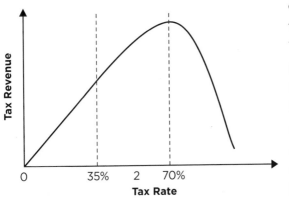

Chapter 9

Why don't we just print more money?

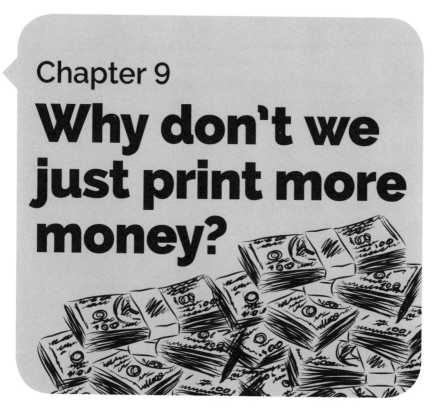

At any point in time there is a fixed amount of money in circulation in an economy. Sometimes, it's not enough.

If a nation doesn't have enough money – perhaps it owes lots in international debt, or its domestic economy is struggling – the question arises, why can't its central bank just print more? After all, it prints money anyway. Then it could use the newly created money to pay off its debts or invest in, say, building roads, houses and schools. In a way, an economy does do this. But it's not quite that straightforward.

Where does money come from?

In the good times, when the economy is healthy, or 'buoyant', more money is steadily created at a relatively low level by banks making loans. Extra money is not made by printing new bank notes and releasing them into circulation, but by creating bank money with no physical existence. For example, if you took out a mortgage for $200,000, the bank would credit your account with $200,000 and you would owe the bank that amount. The two cancel out. Eventually, when you have repaid the debt, the money created for the purposes of the loan disappears again. In the

> *'Whenever a bank makes a loan, it simultaneously creates a matching deposit in the borrower's bank account, thereby creating new money.'*
> Money creation in the modern economy, Bank of England Quarterly Bulletin

meantime, the bank makes real money from the interest you pay for the loan.

Normally, money is created at a steady rate that doesn't cause problems in the economy. But if banks create too much money and there is so much debt that people and businesses can't afford to pay it back, it does become a problem. The banks lose confidence and stop making loans (creating money). The system becomes unbalanced.

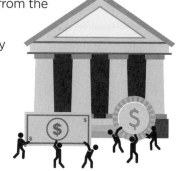

Quantitative easing

In normal times, regulated creation of new money happens through the activities of the commercial banks, overseen by the central bank. In times of crisis, the central bank can create new money through a process called **quantitative easing** (QE). It's considered an 'unconventional' monetary policy, so it's only used in unusual circumstances.

Quantitative easing is not really a licence to print money, because no money is

> **TOO MUCH, TOO FAST**
>
> The Bank of England was formed in 1694. It took over 300 years of moderate lending for banks to create the first trillion pounds ($1.5 trillion). But it took only eight years to create the next trillion.

actually printed – but it's a licence to create money electronically. If the government feels the country would do better if there were more money in circulation, it creates some and then uses it to buy bonds from investors such as insurance companies and pension funds – and so the money slips into the regular economy.

There are two effects. Firstly, the interest paid by the bonds decreases. When interest rates are low, there is no incentive to save, but plenty of incentive to borrow and spend. Borrowing and spending will reinvigorate the economy as the increase in demand stimulates production. Secondly, financial institutions have more money. Since they have extra, they should be more willing to lend it (responsibly, we hope) to businesses that want to grow, or even to people who want to buy a house or a car or a holiday. The businesses produce more goods and services, which people buy because they now have the money. Because businesses have grown, they employ more people, who then have an income to spend. The whole economy becomes more buoyant. The boost to the economy is supposed to lift it out of recession or stagnation.

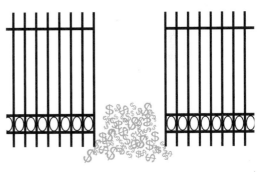

Does it work?

Quantitative easing was first tried by the Bank of Japan in the 1990s, but economists are divided on whether or not it worked. The US has been the most enthusiastic quantitative easer. The Federal Reserve Bank spent $3.7 trillion (£2.4 trillion) on bonds between late 2008 and the start of 2015. It claimed success in reducing unemployment and reaching its target rate of inflation (though it is still very low). The Bank of England bought £200 billion ($300 billion) worth of bonds between March and November 2009 and the economic output of the UK increased by 1.5–2 per cent, which the bank claimed was at least in part a result of QE.

So much for the figures. What do they mean for people? QE invigorates the financial markets rather than the main consumer economy. It is those who own the stocks who benefit first. In the UK, QE boosted share prices by around 20 per cent. As 40 per cent of shares are owned by the richest 5 per cent of the population, the wealthy benefited the most – to the tune of around £128,000 ($196,000) each. The rest of the population benefits through 'trickle down', which relies on the rich spending their (perceived) wealth in ways that boost the economy of their country. It doesn't help much if they buy a yacht from a foreign boat-builder or go abroad on holiday, flying with an airline based in another country. It does help if they spend their money in local restaurants, eating locally grown food, or

use it to buy other goods and services sourced, made or provided in their own country. However, they may spend it on other financial products rather than real goods and services, in which case the trickle down doesn't happen.

Bonds bite back

There is another problem waiting round the corner. Sooner or later the banks will want to sell those bonds they bought. At that point, unless carefully judged and handled, interest rates might rise, and any recovery that QE has spurred could be stifled. When interest rates are low, people will borrow money to buy goods and services and businesses will borrow money to expand. That drives economic activity. When interest rates are high, people don't want to borrow as it costs too much in repayments. They stop buying things, businesses don't borrow to expand and employ people, and the economy becomes less active. It can slump back to where it started.

But, why not *really* print more money?

It might seem that one solution to poverty would be to print more money and just give it to all the people who don't have enough. Why can't we do this?

Suppose a country prints more money so that people in the country can buy more – because they are currently poor and can't afford food or houses, say. Before the new money arrives, a mango costs $1. The country has an economy worth $2 billion. It creates another $2 billion and releases this into the economy. Now many more people can afford to buy mangoes – but mango production hasn't increased. All that happens is that the people selling the mangoes can choose who to sell them to. They do this by putting the price up: competition for goods has increased demand and that leads to increased prices. Soon, mangoes cost $2 instead of $1 and the economy is back where it started: it is no richer because it is not producing any more than it was before.

How about creating money to pay off international debt? That won't work either. Internationally, currencies are not all worth the same. Their value relative to one another fluctuates all the time, representing how much each currency is really 'worth'. If a country prints lots of money, the value of its currency goes down, but its debt does not. The debt is not stored or calculated in each country's own currency. Suppose the imaginary country Utopia had an exchange rate of two Utopian dollars to one US dollar, a debt to the IMF of 5 billion US dollars (or 10 billion Utopian dollars), and a GDP of 10 billion Utopian dollars. Utopia decides to print another 10 billion Utopian dollars to pay off its debt. But now the supply of its currency has doubled, the value of the currency has halved. A $1 mango costs $2 and the international debt of US$5 billion is equal to 20 billion Utopian dollars.

Chapter 10
Don't we still have to make things?

We hear a lot about how we live in a post-industrial age. But do we really? Can we?

We still have lots and lots of stuff. If your bag contains a smart phone, a tablet computer and the electronic key fob for your highly advanced car, you don't seem very post-industrial. But to economists and sociologists 'post-industrial' means that the manufacturing sector of the economy has been overtaken by another, non-industrial sector. Today, the service sector and knowledge economy are larger than the manufacturing sector of the economy in many countries.

From agriculture to industry

Long ago, most people worked in farming. Indeed, even in developed nations, nearly three-quarters of the population worked in agriculture until as recently as the second half of the 19th century. This makes sense, as we can't live without food. The means of production are first employed to meet needs, and then to supply wants once needs have been met. Until the 20th century, agriculture was very labour intensive. Today, in richer countries, only 2–3 per cent of the

population works in agriculture. That has freed labour for other types of production.

Even with most of the population working in farming, agriculture never accounted for more than about half a country's GDP. It's just not very productive in economic terms as food has to be cheap enough for everyone to afford. In richer countries, agriculture now accounts for only 1–2 per cent of GDP. That's not because we aren't growing as much food, though – it's because other contributors to GDP have grown massively.

Leaving the farm

Before agricultural machinery, sowing, weeding, fertilizing and harvesting crops was pretty hard work. But as farming became mechanized people were freed to do other kinds of work, such as manufacturing. In Britain, the change from agriculture to industry began in the Industrial Revolution of the 18th and 19th centuries, when efficient mechanized ploughs, seed-drills (for planting seeds) and hoes took over much manual work. At the same time, the development of mechanization in manufacturing drew redundant farmworkers into cities to work long hours operating machinery.

Another burst of mechanization on farms in the mid-20th century led to a further drop in agricultural work. This was accompanied by a massive growth in manufacturing after the end of World War II, making use of new materials and technologies and serving a newly-wealthy and optimistic population. In the 1950s and 1960s, manufacturing was at its height in Western Europe and the USA, employing nearly 40 per cent of the population.

And leaving the factory

Bending over pulling weeds out of a wheat field is not really a fun way to spend your life. But pulling a lever on a loom or putting chocolates into boxes isn't a lot better. Just as mechanization freed people from backbreaking jobs on farms, so later it freed them from soul-destroying jobs in factories. Mechanizing factories enabled producers to make things much more efficiently and required fewer people, at least in the developed world. Now, in most of the richer nations, only around 10 per cent of people work in manufacturing. Exceptions include Taiwan (28 per cent) and Germany (20 per cent).

In the developing economies, manpower is still a cheap manufacturing resource; many of the goods we buy in developed economies are produced in crowded sweatshops and factories where labour is cheaper than mechanization. Some manufacturing processes are difficult or impossible to mechanize and these, too, are predominantly carried out in areas with a plentiful supply of cheap labour.

Still making things

In the early 1980s, manufacturing was responsible for 57 per cent of world trade; by 1998–2000 it had risen to 78 per cent. In 2009–11 it had fallen again, but was still higher than before at 69 per cent. So manufacturing is still an important economic component, even if fewer people work in it.

With a typical 10 per cent working in manufacturing and 3 per cent in agriculture, a lot of the workforce of a developed country is available for other economic sectors. Many work in service industries: tourism, education, law, medicine, banking, retail and so on.

Service industries don't produce anything new, though they might reconfigure existing things, such as 'adding value' to a cake by selling it in a café on a nice plate. Many service industries are, so far, still quite staff-intensive.

THE 1, 2, 3 OF INDUSTRIES

Primary industries deal in raw materials: digging metals from the ground, drilling for oil and so on.

Secondary industries process raw materials to make things (manufacturing): turning the metal into cars and the wheat into bread and cakes.

Tertiary industries don't produce any physical products, but provide a service: moving the cars around, selling the cakes in cafés, and providing the bank loan to start the café.

Is it really a good idea?

Developed economies have moved a lot of their manufacturing offshore to areas where land and labour are much cheaper, or don't actually manufacture at all, but buy things from manufacturers to sell in western markets. Relatively few clothes or electronic goods, for instance, are made in Western Europe or the USA – most are made in Asia, which has become the 'workshop of the world'.

SAME JOB, DIFFERENT SECTOR

In recent years, many organizations have begun to outsource functions that are not their main business. An example would be a garment factory that outsources its canteen to a catering company and its cleaning to a cleaning company. When people were employed by the garment factory as chefs or cleaners, their jobs were part of the manufacturing sector. Once they are employed by a catering or cleaning company, they are part of the service sector.

Depending on service industries for GDP looked fine when the western economies were doing well. It even had the aura of being clean and sophisticated – none of those grubby factories or poking around in the dirt for us, thank you: we can live by banking, real estate and insurance.

But can we? The financial crash of 2008 demonstrated how vulnerable a service-based economy is. It's particularly vulnerable

when a lot of the services are actually – in most people's terms – illusory: when they involve selling financial 'products' that are barely related to anything in the real world, such as derivatives, futures and reinsurance bundles (see page 266). The recession did not come about because we no longer grew enough food, made enough cars, nursed enough patients in hospitals or ran enough hotels. All those industries were doing exactly what they had done for years and remained productive.

Chapter 11

What are you paying for?

Marketing experts put a lot of effort into setting prices at a level that will encourage people to buy things.

It's not by any means as straightforward as dropping the price. Sometimes raising the price makes people buy things. There is as much psychology and sociology as economics involved in getting pricing right. One important factor is whether people feel they have made the right judgment themselves – pressurizing them rarely works.

You can approach this chapter from the point of view of a buyer or a seller. If you are a buyer, it will make you wise to some of the tricks retailers are trying to play on you. If you're a seller, you could try some of the tricks – they work (at least on people who haven't read about them).

Choosing to pay

People's willingness to pay more or less for goods and services depends on personal criteria that vary, but are combinations of:

- perceived value: does the item deliver features they value?
- utility: how well does the item do what they want it to do?
- quality: is a more expensive item better quality than a cheaper item?
- prestige: will their social standing be enhanced by choosing a more costly item?
- tribal affiliation: is the item a badge of membership of a particular social group?

- availability: is it more difficult to acquire than a cheaper item?
- trust/risk: do they trust the more expensive item to be more reliable, or expect the cheaper one to be a risky purchase that might fall short of expectations in some way?
- ethics: is the expensive item more ethically acceptable (low carbon, organic, for example) or sold by a type of organization they want to support (such as a local independent retailer rather than a chain)?

Buy it, it's cheap!

It's quite common to see items advertised as cheaper than competitors' products. In many markets, you'd expect that to be persuasive – after all, one tin of tomatoes is much the same as another, especially if they're the same brand from a different shop. But it can make people suspicious. If a retailer points out that one product is cheaper than another, customers may suspect that the cheap product is not as good. They start to feel they might be being tricked, or coerced, neither of which they like. They might buy the more expensive option to avoid being cheated or because buying the cheaper option makes them seem penny-pinching or impoverished.

People will buy if they think something is a bargain – that is, cheaper than its true value. If an item is advertised as sale price or reduced, caution disappears. A study at MIT and the University of Chicago found that people were more likely to buy a product if it was marked down from $48 to $40 than if it was full price at $39. As shoppers, though, we have little to go on when trying to determine the value of something: there is an imbalance of information, with the sellers knowing far more about their products than we do.

Confidence tricks

One appeal of auction sites such as eBay is that we can see how much people in general – and not just the retailer – value something, and we take a cue from them. Most people are rather insecure about their own ability to judge value. This leads to caution, particularly where there is an imbalance of information between buyer

ECONOMICS-SPEAK: NET ECONOMIC GAIN

Net economic gain is the value the consumer gains by paying a lower price than they were willing to pay. Assume apples and pears both cost $3 a kilo. You prefer apples and would be willing to pay $4 a kilo for them. For pears, you would only be willing to pay $3.20 a kilo. If you buy a kilo of each for $3, you make $1 net economic gain from the apples (as you have saved $1 you would have been willing to pay), but only 20 cents net economic gain from the pears.

and seller. Someone buying a second-hand car, for example, has much less information about the car they are looking at than the seller has. Consequently, they are likely to be wary, fearing it might have hidden faults, and will be prepared to pay less than if they had confidence in it. On the other hand, if it does turn out later to have faults, they will probably not have dropped their expectations sufficiently and will still pay more than it is worth.

CONTEXT IS ALL

Researchers from Stanford and Rice universities offered two identical CDs on eBay with starting bids of $1.99. One listing was flanked by the same CD auctioned with a starting bid of $0.99 and the other flanked by the same CD starting at $5.99. They found that the CD flanked by more expensive copies always received more bids and went for a higher price than the same CD flanked by cheaper copies. People's perception of the value of the CD was influenced by the other offers.

Then the researchers repeated the test, but this time added text that pointed out the price difference and suggested customers compare the prices. Bidding patterns changed. People waited longer to bid, and the price of the adjacent CDs made no difference to what they were willing to pay. Once the choice to compare was not theirs, they were distrustful and less interested.

Why do people pay more than they have to?

At the opposite end of the scale are those who knowingly pay more than they need to for items. Paying more can often secure better quality, an item with more features, or better sales and after-sales service. People might buy a well-known brand because they have more faith in it – it's a way of reducing the risk of purchasing. But some purchasing decisions go beyond quality and trust.

While a $5 T-shirt might not last as long as a $50 T-shirt, a $500 T-shirt probably won't be any better quality than the $50 T-shirt. You can buy an excellent watch for $500, yet people buy watches that cost $10,000 and more. Adding gold and diamonds to a watch doesn't make it better at keeping the time. So why buy it? People value aesthetic design and will be willing to pay more for things that look good, but not usually to the tune of an extra $9,500. At this point, people are paying for social value – what they think the item says about them.

Prestige and tribal affiliation

Expensive items are like a badge of membership of a social group. This can again be associated with trust and risk, particularly if people trust the judgement of the group they identify with a product, while knowing little about the product and alternatives. Tribal affiliation explains why so many people buy an iPhone without comparing it with other phones on the market, and why there are trends in everything from clothing brands to brands of wine and holiday destinations.

If we don't research the possibilities, if we're insecure about our taste or social position, we'll buy what others are buying if they are people we identify with or aspire to be like. Advertisers cash in on this by showing models using a product in settings that are more glamorous or exotic than those of their target audience. The idea is to make you feel that you, too, will be one of the rich/trendy/attractive/young people if you have this product. You won't – you'll be the same person, with an expensive product.

BUY IT, IT'S EXPENSIVE!

Business psychologist Robert Cialdini cites a jeweller whose turquoise jewellery wasn't selling. She had intended to mark it down to half price, but accidentally marked it as double the price instead. Suddenly, seeing that turquoise jewellery was expensive, people assumed it was special and bought it.

Buy it, we don't want you to!

Most of us have at some point had the experience of going into a shop and being looked down on by snooty shop assistants. We either brazen it out or leave. 'Don't they want me to buy anything?' we grumble internally. Well, no, they don't. If you're not the kind of customer they like to think patronizes the shop, they don't want you in case you diminish their brand. And you probably can't afford it anyway and are just cluttering up the place, putting off the wealthy customers who are less likely to buy the goods if they think 'ordinary' people shop there. It doesn't always work. For some people, being patronized doesn't deter them. The very antipathy of the shop staff adds to the appeal of the product, making it more desirable. These are the **aspirational purchasers** – people who buy because they want to be like the people who have those goods.

The four 'Ps'

Research at the Marshall Business School in California suggests consumers can be divided into four groups according to their attitude to luxury brands. These are: **patricians** (old money), **parvenus** (new money), **poseurs** and **proletarians**.

Patricians buy luxury goods because they want the quality and because of brand loyalty. They are not interested in flashing the label to the general public and will generally pick the non-ostentatious designs that will only be recognized by other patricians.

Parvenus do want to flash the label, as they want to signal to other wealthy people that they are one of the tribe. They're the people who buy Louis Vuitton luggage with the conspicuous logo, the Gucci sunglasses with the prominent Gucci badge, the flashy red Ferrari sports car and distinctive red-soled Louboutin shoes.

Poseurs want to flash the brand, but can't always afford to; they're in the market for cheap lookalike brands and imported fakes that the patricians and parvenus wouldn't touch.

Proletarians don't care about image and just buy what they like and can afford.

The result is that luxury brands such as Gucci and Louis Vuitton often have two types of product – one that is ostentatious and sells to the parvenus and one that is discreet, costs more and sells to the patricians. The cheaper lookalike and 'knock-off' products are predominantly of the parvenu-targeted designs, as that's who the poseurs are emulating.

SILLY MONEY

Who would buy these?
- A gold iPhone for $100,000 (£65,000).
- A gold-and-diamond Bluetooth headset for $50,000 (£32,500)
- Gold staples – yes, staples for paper – for $175 (£113) a packet, though you can get them for $59 (£38) if you shop around.
- A crocodile-skin umbrella for $50,000 (£32,500).
- Diamond-encrusted contact lenses for $15,000 (£9,700) – they're probably not even good for your eyes.

Answer – parvenus!

Desire for status ↓	Wealth →	
	Proletarians	Patricians
	Poseurs	Parvenus

Chapter 12

Why can't I get a job?

Unemployment rates rise and fall – but why?

The traditional pattern of working life was that a person started working – at perhaps 16, 18 or 21, depending on how long they stayed in education – and carried on for 40–50 years, and then retired. But that has become less common. People have periods of unemployment, give up paid work to look after young children or older relatives, retire early (or late), retrain or go back to studying or, in some cases, never work at all.

The need for labour

Labour is one of the factors of production along with land and capital. Without labour, nothing is produced or sold. Even if we imagine a completely automated factory making goods, there will still be people who maintain and repair the machinery, deal with orders and the purchase of raw materials, market the goods – and, perhaps at a different company, make the machines that make the goods. We can't get away from labour. Someone has to do *something*.

The labour market

There is a market for labour, just as there is a market for goods and services and for the other factors of production. It follows the familiar pattern of supply and demand curves (see page 45). When there is a demand for labour, and not enough workers (all together or in a particular sector), wages rise. When there are more people looking for work than there is suitable work for them, wages fall.

Labour is closely tied to human capital, which is the skills and abilities of people, developed through training, education and experience.

Interchangeable jobs and workers

Some types of job demand few skills or personal qualities, so most people would be capable of doing them. For example, cleaning a cinema between showings of films requires someone to walk through the cinema collecting dropped litter and unfinished drinks and clearing away any spills. It is a simple job almost any person with normal mobility and vision could do. This means a huge proportion of the population could do it, though not all will want to.

ECONOMICS-SPEAK: FUNGIBILITY

Items are said to be **fungible** if they are easily interchanged. They are not fungible if they are unique. For instance, cartons of semi-skimmed milk are fungible: each carton is the same as another, and you could exchange them with no effect. Original works of art are not fungible – each is very different, with a different value and unique history. Jobs and workers vary widely in fungibility depending on the nature of the work. Generally, unskilled jobs are fungible and skilled jobs less so.

There are also many other jobs that don't require skills and training. Let's suppose a person with no training wants an unskilled job and there are two jobs available with the same rates of pay: one is picking fruit on a farm, and the other is picking up litter in a cinema. They might apply to the cinema because they will get to see some movies, and perhaps the hours fit better with their other commitments (such as looking after children). Or they might apply to the farm because they prefer to work outdoors. If either the cinema or farm finds it cannot attract workers it might decide to increase the wages on offer. Then applicants have to decide which is more important to them: better pay or being outside/seeing movies at work?

Too few workers: demand for labour

In a market where there are fewer workers willing to do a job than there are jobs, employers are forced to offer more incentives in order to attract staff. This might include more pay, more flexible working hours, or extra benefits (free fruit from the farm, perhaps). The demand for labour in any industry is affected by:

- **the price of other factors of production:** if the price of automation drops, workers will be replaced by machines

- **increasing efficiency:** if working practices become more productive, fewer workers are needed
- **demand for goods:** if demand rises, the demand for labour increases in order to raise supply.

The labour market, like any other, follows the rules of supply and demand. Extra incentives attract new workers to the market. Perhaps higher wages mean people can afford childcare or transport, enabling them to take a job, or older people delay retirement to earn more. As more people enter the market, the supply of workers rises, so the higher demand is met. Wages don't need to rise any further. If they did rise further, people in skilled jobs might decide to take a more boring job in exchange for better pay, so the pool of workers would grow quickly. Remember, these are jobs almost anyone can do if they choose to.

Markets are linked. If the wage that a cinema has to pay cleaners rises too high, the price of cinema tickets will have to rise to cover the cost. Then fewer people will go to the cinema, fewer cleaners will be needed, and wages will fall again.

Too many workers: supply of labour

Now suppose the market is not buoyant for workers. There are few unskilled jobs available. The supply of labour is affected by:

- **population change:** a rise in the birthrate will lead to a later bulge in the working population, and a fall in the birthrate will lead to few workers being available later. The same change in population might affect the demand for goods, so there might be no effect on wages.

- **migration:** if workers move from one area to another to find work, more labour will be available and wages are likely to fall.
- **tax rates:** the marginal benefits of working are affected by tax rates. People might not be keen to work extra hours if the tax arrangements mean they will gain little or no extra cash as a result.

When the supply of labour is good, employers don't need to offer extra incentives. They can offer low wages and still fill the vacancies. How low can it go? This depends on the situation in any particular country and whether the government intervenes in the labour market. Some countries have a legal minimum wage and all employers must pay at least this amount. Some have a welfare system that will support people who are out of work, or top up the earnings of people in low-paid jobs. Generous welfare support means that people might choose not to work for a low wage if they can get as much from state benefits. Employers will have to pay more to attract workers. If a government provides subsidies for people in low-paid work, the employer can pay low wages knowing the government will top up the workers' income. If there is no regulation and no welfare back-up, employers can get away with paying very low wages and forcing people to work very long hours. Most developed economies have introduced legislation setting out minimum pay and conditions to try to prevent the exploitation of workers, but some businesses get round this by outsourcing to places where no such laws apply (or where they are not enforced).

Scarcity: skills shortage

It is not always the case that any particular individual will have difficulty finding a job in times of high unemployment. Even during an economic downturn, some skills might be in high demand while there is a surplus of other types of worker.

Despite high general unemployment in many economies, employers sometimes grumble that they can't find the staff they need. This often applies to people with specialist skills such as engineers or surgeons. These jobs command high wages because they are difficult to do, and employees have invested time, effort and perhaps money in learning to do them. They want to be rewarded for their investment by earning more than an unskilled worker. At the same time, it is not a simple matter for an unemployed person to retrain as an engineer or surgeon, so the high demand does not rapidly lead to an increase in supply.

Other factors

The labour market is complicated by factors other than money. A person with a burning ambition to become a vet is unlikely to train in accountancy instead just because there are more jobs for accountants. A person who wants to be a musician, but has the qualifications to become an engineer, might still choose to be a musician and earn less than they could as an engineer. They might even take an unskilled job to support themselves while trying to carve out a career in music. The personal satisfaction they gain from being a musician is more important to them than money or job security.

Another problem is that the school or college system in place in a particular country might not produce potential candidates with the qualifications or skills that employers demand. Employers may then feel the need to train new recruits themselves, which is both costly and time-consuming. There might, for example, be low levels of IT-literacy among school-leavers, or more people with management qualifications than there are vacancies, but fewer with the foreign-language skills needed for international trade. People who can speak Chinese or Arabic may be in short supply, in which case an English-speaker who can conduct business negotiations in one of these languages will be more in demand than a monoglot English speaker.

People need to live

Unlike other factors of production, workers have additional needs, such as affordable accommodation, schooling for their children, reliable transport to work and so on. These needs have an impact on the labour market. For example, high housing costs

> ### TRAIN AND RUN
> Training staff is costly. Once staff are qualified, some might leave and work for a competitor, especially if they are offered better rates of pay. In fact, if the competitor is not paying for training, they might well be able to afford to pay higher wages. They can save their training budget by poaching staff who have been trained at another employer's expense. To get round this problem, some employers use contracts that tie trainees to a minimum period of employment or require them to repay training costs if they leave too soon after qualifying.

can force both skilled and unskilled workers to move away from an area. In this case, wages will have to rise, and/or housing and transport costs will have to fall to avoid creating a labour shortage. For many cities around the world, this is already a major issue. Governments must then decide whether to intervene and, for example, provide low-cost social housing, subsidized public transport, and increased provision for schooling and healthcare to draw workers back into the cities.

Mobility of labour

The supply of labour is affected by the mobility of labour. Mobility in relation to the labour force has two aspects: geographical mobility and occupational mobility.

Geographical mobility refers to people being willing and able to move in order to take work. This is the type of mobility demonstrated by Norman Tebbit's father moving south to look for work in the 1930s

GET ON YOUR BIKE

In the late 1970s the decline in heavy industry in the north of England led to mass unemployment. In the summer of 1981, rioting broke out in the largest cities – Liverpool, Manchester, Birmingham and London. Norman Tebbit MP, who became Employment Secretary in September of 1981, rejected the suggestion that rioting was a natural response to the situation, saying: 'I grew up in the '30s with an unemployed father. He didn't riot. He got on his bike and looked for work, and he kept looking till he found it.'

This was frequently misquoted as Tebbit telling unemployed people to get on their bikes and find work, and he was afterwards referred to as 'Onyerbike'. His father's strategy of getting on his bike and looking for work is a demonstration of the mobility of labour.

(see box on page 159), and by the large number of Eastern European workers who have moved into Western Europe following the fall of the Soviet Union. As plumbers, electricians and other skilled workers moved west, they easily found employment because they were willing to work longer hours for lower wages than western workers in the same trades.

Occupational mobility refers to people's willingness and ability to change professions – from hairdresser to swimming instructor, for instance. Within the unskilled and semi-skilled labour market, this is relatively easy. For skilled jobs, it is difficult, time-consuming and costly because the necessary skills take longer to acquire. Workers might not be willing or able to retrain for a different type of job.

When Tebbit's father moved from the north to the south of England he had to find a different kind of work, as the heavy industries such as steelmaking and coalmining that were closing down in the north were not available in the south. He therefore demonstrates both types of mobility – occupational and geographical – by changing skill and changing location.

Government intervention

Direct government intervention and changes to legislation can also affect the job market.

If a government sets a minimum wage (the lowest wage employers are allowed to pay), the short-term effect may be that job vacancies fall and unemployment rises. But experience in Europe suggests that in the longer term a minimum wage can increase the demand for labour. A higher wage means both employers and workers are investing more in the job and productivity increases as a result.

Legislation that gives employers more costs or responsibilities – such as a company pension – might result in staff cutbacks. If the government offers subsidies to employers, perhaps to take on school leavers or people with disabilities, that might lead to more jobs for certain groups of workers. Similarly, if government relaxes regulations over pay and conditions or reduces the financial burden of employing people, demand for labour is likely to rise.

The labour market is also affected by anti-discrimination laws, which increase the labour pool (the number of available workers), by subsidized childcare (making more parents available for work) and by encouraging or subsidizing training schemes. Relaxing or tightening controls on immigration can also affect the labour market as it increases or reduces the number of foreign workers available to employers.

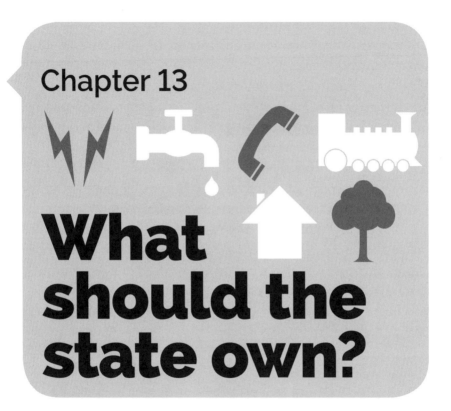

Chapter 13

What should the state own?

In some countries, vital utilities, industries and infrastructure are owned by the state; in others, they are in private hands.

All governments accept that some goods and services are essential. These include clean drinking water, gas and electricity, military defence, a police and judicial system and so on. But governments take different views on how they should be provided. Should they be state owned or privately owned? Should they be run as a monopoly, with fixed prices, or should free-market forces determine the costs? In some countries with free-market economies, utilities such as gas and electricity are state owned, whereas in other countries they are privately owned. Such decisions tend to be made on political as much as economic grounds.

Types of good

Economists distinguish between **public goods** and **private goods**. Confusingly, 'goods' in this case is not the same as 'goods' that are distinct from services; this time, goods include services and are anything that brings benefit to someone.

Private goods are those that are limited in supply and from which people can be excluded. If something is limited in supply, its use by one person prevents its use by another. If I buy a pizza and eat it, it's gone for good and no one else can have it. This makes it a **rivalrous good**: people are rivals in consumption.

Private goods are also **excludable**: people can be excluded from the use of them. People can only go to the cinema to see a movie if they pay for a ticket. Without a ticket, they are excluded.

Public goods are **non-rivalrous** and **non-excludable**. This means that use by one person doesn't prevent use by another, and people can't be excluded from benefiting from it. Examples include street lighting, national defence and firework displays. The fact that one person is able to make use of street lighting, or enjoy the fireworks, doesn't prevent others from doing so. Similarly, no one can be excluded from the benefit of national defence, street lighting or seeing fireworks. Not only can people not be excluded – they often can't choose to exclude themselves. Many public goods are non-refusable. People can't individually refuse a national space programme or fluoride added to drinking water.

Semi-public or **quasi-public goods** have some elements of public goods, but are not entirely private goods. Use of a library is excludable: people without a library card are not allowed to borrow books from the library. Even though the library might be paid for from taxes and the card might be issued without any charge, people can be excluded from using the library if they don't have a card. But it's not rivalrous – one person using the library doesn't stop another using it. Some goods are semi-public because they can become rivalrous. For example, a road network can be semi-public if there are tolls on some bridges or roads, and a beach can be semi-public if at peak times it is so busy there is not space for more visitors.

Free-riders

Many goods that a state needs to provide are either public or semi-public. Non-excludable goods present a problem for the state as they can't be provided only to the people who pay for them and withheld from others. This leads to the problem of **free-riders**: people who benefit from a good, but don't contribute to its cost.

Imagine a country, Neutopia, which wants a free-market economy. The government believes that people should choose how to spend their money. Few of them want to make a contribution to paying for sewers, an army, a police force and street lighting, though. Indeed, the people of Neutopia would probably not even pay to have a government. Most just want to enjoy themselves – having holidays, enjoying evenings out and owning fast cars. As they have limited financial resources, if they had to choose between paying for military equipment for the army and buying a new car for themselves, most would buy a new car. They soon realize that the goods they don't want to pay for are non-excludable; they still benefit from having a police force or a sewerage system, even if they don't pay for it themselves. Too many free-riders would cause problems.

To start with, everything might look fine. But with no money to pay for public services, it would not be long before criminals took advantage of the lack of a police force, and the place became very smelly and unhealthy because there was no sewerage system. If it is left to the free market to provide these goods, there is no guarantee they will be provided to an adequate standard. So governments recognize that – however strong their commitment to free-market principles – there are some things that the public must pay for

whether they like it or not. The way they get people to pay for public services is through taxation (see page 114 – *Why do we pay taxes?*).

Merit goods

Some public goods, and some private goods, are also classed as **merit goods**. These are good for society as a whole. They include education, healthcare, sports facilities, museums, libraries and public broadcasting. If merit goods were left entirely to the free market there is no guarantee private companies would provide sufficient facilities for all those who need them at a price they can afford. As they benefit the whole of society, most governments choose to provide at least some merit goods free or cheaply at the point of use.

It might seem that the person who benefits from education or vaccination is the person who is educated or vaccinated. In fact, the whole of society benefits from having a better-educated population, who generally become more productive workers and so trigger economic growth. Similarly, the whole of society benefits from herd immunity if most of the population is vaccinated, as it reduces the risk that infectious diseases spread – there are simply too few vulnerable people for a disease to take hold in a population.

Demerit goods

The opposite of merit goods are **demerit goods**. These are over-provided by the market and harmful to society. Examples are street drugs, alcohol and tobacco products. Governments can intervene in several ways. They can ban the demerit good (as they do with street drugs); they can use taxes to increase the price of the goods and so reduce consumption (as with tobacco and alcohol); and they can use education and campaigns to discourage people from buying and using it.

Paying for things you don't want

There are several reasons a government might decide to make people pay for something they would not personally choose to pay for, and different ways of doing it. For example, people might be forced or persuaded to pay for education (for their children or others), car insurance, a pension fund or health insurance.

Governments can use taxation or legislation to ensure that people pay. It's a legal requirement to take out car insurance if you want to drive on the roads, for example, to guarantee that you can compensate other road users if you have an accident and injure them or damage their car. It might be a legal requirement to pay into a fund for a pension or health insurance, or the money might be taken from your income. A government might use advertising and public information campaigns to try to persuade people to pay into a pension fund, or make vaccination a legal requirement for children before they can register at a school.

Who does the work?

Once a local or national government body has decided which public goods and services to provide, it must choose how to provide them. It can employ staff itself or contract out to private firms to provide the service. It is not economic for a government to keep all the staff it may ever need permanently on its books. Local authorities do not employ people to repair roads, for example. Instead they pay a private company to do this as and when needed. On the other hand, schools require a certain number of teachers on a permanent basis, so teachers will be directly employed by the local authority all year round.

Should we privatize essential industries?

Views on how many and which services should be provided by the state vary, and as governments change, so does state provision. The more an economy tends towards a free market, the more essential services will be privately owned. Some that were previously state owned might be sold to private investors. The UK government has sold off many state-owned services in the past 50 years, including British Gas, British Telecom, the Post Office and British Rail. The argument put forward to justify privatization is that services will be run more efficiently and competitively in the private sector and this will benefit consumers. In fact, many of the privatized services in the UK are now largely owned by state-run enterprises based overseas, as they have been able to buy shares in them on the open market. Much of the profit these businesses make goes overseas to state-run organizations or to shareholders, so is not reinvested for the benefit of UK consumers.

Whereas right-leaning governments tend to favour privatization, left-leaning governments are likely to bring more services into state or public ownership and might even re-nationalize industries that had previously been sold to the private sector. One example is the UK rail network infrastructure (such as tracks, stations and signals), which was originally privately owned, then brought into public ownership, then privatized again, and has since been re-nationalized. Neither private nor public ownership has proved more efficient.

Privatized or public?

Advantages of privatization	Disadvantages of privatization
Improved efficiency as private firms seek to maximize profit by cutting costs	Fall in standards as economic considerations are put ahead of quality of service
Ability to take a long-term view: those in charge are not restricted to an elected term in office	The wishes of shareholders may take precedence over the needs of employees, the business itself and consumers of the service. For example, shareholders hope for high dividends (pay-outs on their shares), and might vote for this instead of buying new trains or pipelines that would improve the service in the long term.

Increased competition benefits consumers if it leads to falling prices and rising standards	In the case of natural monopolies, such as water companies, lack of competition and state regulation can lead to consumer exploitation (such as higher prices but poorer service) as consumers have no alternative
Lack of political interference; a state-run organization might be reluctant to cut staff, for instance, because of the political fall-out	Can lead to fragmentation, with some areas of responsibility or parts of the market being overlooked or neglected
The sale of shares in the organization raises funds for the state	It is a one-off injection of cash, and the state benefits little (only in taxes) from any profit the organization makes later

Many economists feel that privatization is a valid option for industries in which there is no natural monopoly and where free-market competition will ensure prices are kept down and standards kept high. Telecoms is an example of a service that can be provided by many alternative suppliers in a competitive market with few adverse effects on the service. Water supply is a natural monopoly, however. There is no opportunity for consumer choice, so no market-driven incentive for suppliers to lower prices or raise standards.

Chapter 14

Is inflation good or bad?

No shopper likes rising prices. But prices that don't rise at all are a bad sign for the economy.

Inflation is a sustained rise in general prices over time; it reduces the **purchasing power** of money. It means that a dollar, pound or euro will buy less today than it did last year. For example, if you have $1 and a chocolate bar costs $0.99, you can buy one. If inflation pushes the price up to $1.01, that chocolate bar has become unaffordable – sad, but true.

A basket of good(ie)s

Inflation is measured within an economy, showing how prices change over time. As the price of individual items is affected by many factors, inflation is measured by tracking the price of a selection of goods and services that households typically buy. These goods are generally called a **basket**, **market basket** or **consumer bundle**. The basket represents the type of things that the average person is likely to buy. So, in the UK, popular staples and essentials such as bacon, tea, bread, milk and petrol have been included in the basket right from the start. Items are chosen to reflect their importance in people's spending patterns at any given moment. But these change over time, so particular goods and services may be added to or dropped from the consumer basket as fashions (or purchasing patterns) alter. In 2015, for instance, yoghurt drinks and sat navs were dropped. Sweet potatoes and subscriptions to streaming music channels (Spotify, for example) were added to the basket.

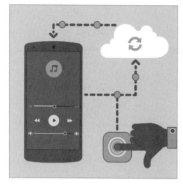

This represents the declining popularity of yoghurt drinks and sat navs and the increasing popularity of sweet potatoes and Spotify. The basket also includes typical amounts for utility bills; transport costs, such as rail season tickets; entertainments such as cable TV subscriptions and cinema tickets; child-minding and care-home costs; one-off large purchases, such as holidays, cars and fridges, and so on. When the UK basket was introduced in 1947, it contained 150 items; by 2015, the number had risen to over 700.

INSIGHT INTO OUR LIVES

Looking at items entering and leaving the basket gives an intriguing insight into everyday life. In 1952, the washing machine made its first appearance, and ten years later the mangle was dropped. The breadbin went in 2001 and the VHS recorder in 2007. The mobile phone was added in 2005 and a garden bird feeder in 2014.

Consumer price index

By monitoring the changing price of the basket, we can tell whether prices in general are rising or falling. This is called the **consumer price index** (CPI). Imagine that in one year the price of goods in the basket was €300. We will call this Year 0. The following year (Year 1) the price was €330, and the year after (Year 2) it was €390.

To calculate CPI, we need a base year; let's take Year 0 as the base. CPI is calculated as

$$\frac{\textbf{Cost in current year}}{\textbf{Cost in base year}} \text{ x 100}$$

So for the base year (Year 0):

$$\frac{£300}{£300} \text{ x 100 = 100}$$

For the next year (Year 1):

$$\frac{£330}{£300} \text{ x 100 = 110}$$

And for the following year (Year 2):

$$\frac{£390}{£300} \text{ x 100 = 130}$$

The CPI is 100, 110 and 130 respectively. The inflation rate is calculated from the difference in CPI between two years, so the inflation rate over the first year (Year 0 to Year 1) is 110 – 100 = 10 per cent. The inflation rate over the next year (Year 1 to Year 2) is 130 – 110 = 20 per cent.

This nation is heading for bad times

Like any tool, CPI has its limitations. For one thing, it fails to take account of the intelligence and autonomy of consumers who will adjust their purchasing as prices change. If apples become very expensive, consumers will buy fewer apples and more of another fruit. If breakfast cereal becomes very cheap, consumers might buy more of that and fewer croissants. This is called **substitution bias**; people will seek to cut their expenditure by substituting one item for another. Changes in the quality of goods and services are also not reflected. For example, if technological changes improve the quality of an item in the basket but the price stays the same, this is of benefit to the consumer but the CPI does not reflect this.

THE LOO ROLL INDEX

Economists have found correlations between particular products or choices and consumer confidence. For example, sales of luxury loo rolls are an indicator of confidence in the economic market. People feel they can afford a small luxury when they are confident their income won't fall. In 1962, economist George Taylor introduced the Hemline Index, plotting the length of women's skirts against income: shorter skirts require more spending on tights or stockings and reflect a buoyant economy. Short hairstyles are also a sign of prosperity as they cost more to maintain.

Why do prices go up?

Economists often focus on two causes of inflation: **cost-push** and **demand-pull**.

Cost-push inflation occurs when the costs associated with production rise (wages, taxes, cost of imports and raw materials). As the cost of manufacturing or supplying a service rises, the price of the product must also rise if the business is to carry on making a profit. So rising costs push up prices.

Demand-pull inflation happens when there is more demand for goods and services than can be met by the available supply. Producers can then demand a higher price and, being opportunistic, they do so. This happens when an economy is growing, people have more money to spend and their demands can't be met by supply.

Bad effects

It's easy to see why people don't like inflation. Things cost more; the

same amount of money buys us less. Life is not as much fun when you can't afford things. On the whole, though, wages rise with inflation, so the effect on most people is marginal unless inflation is either unexpected or gets out of hand.

The people who suffer most when inflation hits are those living on a fixed income or savings. The value of savings is eroded by inflation as the same amount of saved money buys less.

Going down . . .

In general, inflation is seen to be a sign of a flourishing economy: demand-pull inflation suggests that people are prosperous. During

WHERE DO THE STAGS COME INTO IT?

The term **stagflation** is a portmanteau word built from *stag*nation and in*flation*. There are no stags, sadly. The **stag**nation of the market means there is little economic growth and generally high unemployment. At the same time, in**flation** is high. It's not a good condition. With unemployment high and no growth, income doesn't keep pace with prices and so the standard of living drops – people can no longer afford to buy as many things with their income. Stagflation happened in the 1970s in the developed world when an oil crisis started in the Middle East and pushed the price of fuel up. This meant that the prices of most goods also rose (as the cost of products such as plastic made from oil, all forms of transport used to move them, and heating and electricity generation also went up). As price rises were not accompanied by growth, wages did not rise in line with inflation and people became poorer.

the recent years of economic turmoil, inflation has been low, even non-existent. The opposite of inflation is **deflation** – it happens when prices fall.

That sounds like a benefit, as it means we can buy more stuff for the same money. But economists and politicians don't like deflation. It is generally caused by a drop in the supply of money or credit, meaning that people can't afford to buy so much. As a result, prices drop to try to entice people to spend more. Deflation can lead or contribute to recession or depression. As buying stalls and prices drop, profits on the sales that are made also fall, and businesses might have to lay off staff and cut back on production. Higher unemployment means people have even less money to spend, so demand drops further. The economy falls into a vicious circle of decreasing demand leading to lower prices, which in turn leads to lower profits, then lower employment, and so to a further decrease in demand and spending.

A period of deflation occurred in Japan in the early 1990s. The Japanese government dropped interest rates to zero to try to boost spending, but it did not have the desired rapid effect and it took until 2006 for the Japanese economy to start to recover. Europe and the USA tried to avoid deflation in the 2010s through quantitative easing – producing more money to release into the economy to boost spending (see page 124 – *Why don't we just print more money?*).

Too much money

Too much inflation can be worse than too little.

Hyperinflation occurs when prices rise out of all control. The most famous historical example of hyperinflation occurred in the German Weimar Republic between 1921 and 1924. Germany had financed World War I with debt, and as a consequence the international value of its currency had fallen from 4.2 marks to the US dollar, at the start of the war, to 32 marks at the end of 1919. Crippled by the need to pay reparations for World War I in gold or foreign currency, Germany needed to purchase foreign money at any cost, so printed more and more marks in order to do so. The result was that the value of the mark fell even further – to 330 marks/dollar by the end of 1921. Conferences in 1922 held to try to deal with the reparations crisis failed and the mark went into freefall and hyperinflation. By December 1922, the exchange rate was 800 marks to the dollar – just eleven months later this had risen to more than 4.2 trillion marks to the dollar. The wholesale price index (1 in the base year of 1914) was 726 billion by November 1923. Notes were printed in denominations of hundreds of millions, then billions, and finally trillions – the largest

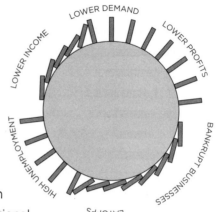

LOWER DEMAND
LOWER INCOME
LOWER PROFITS
HIGH UNEMPLOYMENT
BANKRUPT BUSINESSES
LAYOFFS

denomination note printed was 100 trillion marks. By the end of the crisis in late 1923, 300 paper mills and 150 printing companies using 2,000 presses worked day and night to print currency.

The effect on the German people was catastrophic. Any money held before hyperinflation was worthless – the price of a house would not buy a loaf of bread. As soon as people realized their money was losing value, they started to spend it rapidly. That drove prices up further, increasing the rate of inflation. To start with, the wealthy moved their money into art, gold, jewellery and real estate, but then ordinary people bought things – *any* things. An alternative economy based on barter grew up. It had to – a loaf of bread cost 200 billion marks in November 1923, and an egg cost 80 billion – 500 billion times the cost in 1914.

'At 11:00 in the morning a siren sounded, and everybody gathered in the factory forecourt, where a five-ton lorry was drawn up loaded brimful with paper money. The chief cashier and his assistants climbed up on top. They read out names and just threw out bundles of notes. As soon as you had caught one you made a dash for the nearest shop and bought just anything that was going.'
Willy Derkow, a German student in 1923

Not worth the paper it's printed on

As the situation deteriorated, people had to move money about in wheelbarrows. Now-worthless banknotes were used as wallpaper, or given to children to cut up as craft paper, as they were worth less than real toys. Photos record people burning bundles of notes in stoves, as they were of less value than firewood.

Workers were paid in cash at the start of the day and given half an hour in which to spend their wages before they became worthless; some were paid three times a day, and passed money to relatives waiting at the factory gates to take it away to spend. The price of a cup of coffee doubled in the time it took to drink it. Waiters stood on tables and announced revised prices for the menu every half hour.

Fixed

The situation was finally resolved in November 1923 by the introduction of a new currency, the Rentenmark. As there was no gold to back the currency, it was backed by land used for agriculture and business. The land was mortgaged to the tune of 3.2 billion marks in 1913, and so 3.2 billion Rentenmark were issued. The value of one Rentenmark was 4.2 US dollars (the value of the mark before World War I) and was exchanged at the rate of one Rentenmark to one trillion old marks.

Worse than very bad

German hyperinflation was very bad, but the experience of Zimbabwe was even worse. The Zimbabwean dollar, introduced in 1980, underwent three official redenominations; by the end, one fourth-generation dollar was worth 10^{25} first generation dollars (that's a '1' followed by 25 zeros). In April 2009, the Zimbabwean currency was officially abandoned and all transactions in Zimbabwe carried out in foreign currencies including the US dollar, South African rand, pound sterling, euro, rupee and Chinese yuan.

Setting the price of porridge

As too much inflation and too little inflation are both a sign of an unhealthy economy, governments aim at a 'Goldilocks zone' of just the right amount of inflation, generally considered to be around 2–3 per cent. This allows controlled growth of the economy, without prices outstripping wages, and enough demand to keep suppliers extending their output.

Chapter 15

If we are the 99 per cent, who are the 1 per cent?

It's a well-known truism now that the poor are getting poorer and the rich are getting richer.

Inequality is the plague of modern economies. Canadian economist Chrystia Freeland points out that while even the wealthiest people are willing to think about how to tackle poverty, most people are wary of talking about inequality. We can tackle poverty by giving money to the poor – even a little bit helps. But to tackle inequality some of us have to recognize that we have too much compared with the people who have too little, and that's uncomfortable.

Economists consider inequality in three ways:

- difference in income
- difference in wealth
- difference in consumption.

The growing gap

In the 1970s, the top 1 per cent of the US population accounted for around 10 per cent of the national income. Now, they account for more than 20 per cent of the national income. But the very top 0.1 per cent of the population has increased its share to 8 per cent of the income – almost as much as the top 1 per cent held 40 years previously. In 2005, the wealth of Warren Buffet and Bill Gates was equivalent to the wealth of the bottom 40 per cent of the US population (120 million people). It's not only a problem in the USA. The effect is most marked in the capitalist countries that are closest to a free-market model. The UK is approaching the USA in wealth inequality. Over the whole world, according to figures released by Oxfam in 2014, 1 per cent of the population owns 46 per cent of the wealth, and the richest 85 individuals own as much as the poorest half of the world's population (3.5 billion people).

Now you see it . . .

In 2007, Americans already saw their country as being divided into two classes: the haves and the have-nots. But few people were quite aware of just how divided the nation had become.

In 2014, a survey asked people what they thought the relationship between bosses' pay and employees' pay actually was – and what

THE MOST UNEQUAL

The richest person who has ever lived is Carlos Slim Helú, a Mexican corporate magnate who owns a large number of businesses in many different sectors from civil engineering and telecoms to music and healthcare. His holdings account for around 40 per cent of the Mexican stock exchange. His personal fortune was listed by Forbes in 2014 as $81.6 billion (£53 billion); he has given away $4 billion (£2.6 billion) to philanthropic causes (5 per cent of his wealth).

it should be. On average, they thought it was about 30:1 and should be around 8:1, but some estimates for the actual ratio were as much as 354:1. The average CEO's pay was around $12 million (£7.8m) and the average employee's pay around $34,000 (£22,000). In the 1960s, the typical American CEO earned around 20 times as much as the average employee, so the ratio has increased by a factor of 17.

The situation is not as bad elsewhere, but neither is it healthy:

	Actual ratio	What people think it is	What people think it should be
Poland	28:1	13.3	5
Denmark	48:1	3.7	2
Japan	67:1	10	6
Israel	76:1	7	3.6
UK	84:1	13.5	5.3
Australia	93:1	40	8.3
France	104:1	24.2	6.7
Spain	127:1	6.7	3
Germany	147:1	16.7	6.3
Switzerland	148:1	12.3	5
USA	354:1	29.6	6.7

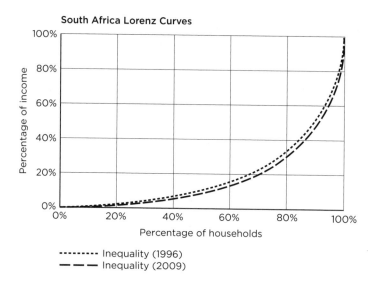

South Africa Lorenz Curves

- - - - - - - - Inequality (1996)
— — — Inequality (2009)

Drawing inequality

The Lorenz curve plots cumulative percentage of the population against cumulative percentage of income or wealth. This means that at the lefthand side, a tiny percentage of the population has earned a tiny percentage of the income, and at the righthand side all the population has earned all the income. It's easy to see how unequal a society is by reading off the percentage earned or owned by, say, the bottom 10 per cent or top 20 per cent.

This shows that in 2009 South Africa was a very unequal society; the bottom 20 per cent of households earned less than 5 per cent of the income in the whole country, whereas the top 10 per cent of households earned more than 50 per cent of the income.

Drawing a straight line at 45 degrees from zero people/income to 100 per cent people/income shows how the curve would look in a perfectly equitable society, in which everyone earned the same. Along the straight line, 20 per cent of the people earn 20 per cent of the income, 50 per cent of the people earn 50 per cent of the income and so on – each percentage point of people earns a percentage point of the income.

The Gini coefficient of inequality

In this diagram the difference between the straight line and the Lorenz curve represents the level of inequality in a society. By measuring the area under the Lorenz curve and the area under the straight line, we can compare the two, giving a measure of inequality known as the Gini coefficient. It was developed by the Italian economist

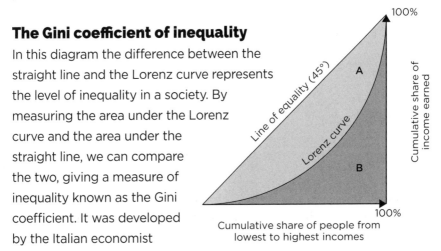

Cumulative share of people from lowest to highest incomes

> *'We have no paupers. The great mass of our population is of laborers; our rich, who can live without labor, either manual or professional, being few, and of moderate wealth. Most of the laboring class possess property, cultivate their own lands, have families, and from the demand for their labor are enabled to exact from the rich and the competent such prices as enable them to be fed abundantly, clothed above mere decency, to labor moderately and raise their families. Can any condition of society be more desirable than this?'*
> Thomas Jefferson (1814)

Corrado Gini in 1912. The Gini coefficient is expressed as a number between 0 and 1 (or sometimes between 0 and 100) and shows how the actual Lorenz curve differs from the perfectly equitable position (the straight line graph).

G (gini coefficient) = A ÷ (A + B)

A Gini coefficient of 0 means an equal economy in which everyone earns or owns the same amount. A coefficient of 1 denotes absolute inequality, where everything is owned or earned by one person.

Who is more and who is less equal?

Using the Gini coefficient as a measure of inequality, the most unequal country in the world was until recently South Africa, with a coefficient of 0.65 in 2011 (World Bank figure). At the same time, China had a Gini coefficient of 0.37 and the USA of about 0.41. Most major economies have a Gini coefficient between 0.3 and 0.5.

The coefficient differs according to whether it is calculated before or after taking account of taxes and welfare benefits. As these attempt to make society more equal, the coefficient is generally lower if they are taken into account. For example, France's Gini coefficient of 0.485 is reduced to 0.293 after taxes; the UK goes from 0.456 to 0.345, so the UK tax system is not as good at creating equality as the French system. The USA has a pre-tax Gini coefficient almost the same as that of France, at 0.486, but taxation does not reduce it as much: it is still 0.380 after taxes.

How did we get here?

Inequality has become much worse very quickly. Economists cite several reasons for this including: globalization, increasing use of technology, and neo-liberal politics.

Globalization has emerged naturally as technology and transport have improved. Corporations are no longer restricted to local or national markets for their goods but can sell them around the whole world easily. There is now a global market of around a billion middle-class people with money to spare. With the economies of scale that come from making much larger quantities, manufacturers' production costs are lower per item. They can often make goods more cheaply, too, by building factories close to the source of raw materials and in countries where labour is cheap. Increased profits go to the shareholders, making them richer.

Technology also makes it possible to produce more items with fewer workers. The balance of the means of production shifts from labour to capital. As less is spent on labour and more on buying technology, more money goes to other large corporations and less to individual workers. Again, money accumulates with the owners.

Neo-liberal politics favours the market and so helps business owners more than workers. Recent policies that have contributed to inequality include:

Deregulation: reducing the restrictions on what corporations can do, giving them more freedom to act for profit rather than in the interests of workers, the environment or the population.

Privatization of previously state-owned industries and resources (see page 169): moving ownership and management of these into private hands leads to them generating profit for shareholders rather than benefiting the whole population.

Lower taxes: intended to encourage investment in industry and entrepreneurship, one effect is that high earners keep more of their income and spending on public goods is reduced because the government has less tax revenue to spend.

Less protection for unionized workers: there is more freedom in the market if workers can't distort it through grouping together to make demands, such as higher wages or better working conditions.

NEO-LIBERALISM

The term neo-liberal first appeared in the 1930s to describe a 'third way' between the laissez-faire capitalism of the 19th century and the socialist command economies. It fell out of use for a while, and re-emerged in the 1980s as a label for the very right-wing, market-driven economic approach of General Augusto Pinochet in Chile. The economic theorists F.A. Hayek and Milton Friedman promoted a move towards maximizing the free market and reducing government intervention, an approach adopted by Ronald Reagan in the USA and Margaret Thatcher in the UK. Friedman's neo-liberal policy of monetarism, which puts control of the money supply at its centre, has been blamed by many economists for the 2007–8 financial crash.

Finally, a cultural shift has made us more tolerant of wide disparities in income. As the gap between rich and poor has widened, it has also been normalized.

Is it really a problem?

The very wealthy often defend their case by saying that they generate wealth and so are entitled to the lion's share of the profits they make. Some say they should not be obliged to pay taxes, because wealth generation itself benefits society and in addition many wealthy people aid the poor through charitable donations (referring to the tradition of philanthropy among many wealthy Americans). Morality and entitlement are certainly worth debating, but a more objective point is that high levels of inequality are destabilizing and can't be sustained in the long term. Many economic arguments suggest that capitalism will undermine itself if allowed to create unchecked inequality.

Limiting factors

The idea that unchecked inequality will lead to disaster is not new. In the 19th century, the English political economist David Ricardo and the political philosopher Karl Marx both considered that a small elite group would take an ever-increasing share of all that was produced. In Ricardo's case, it was the landowners who fulfilled this role; for Marx it was the factory owners, the industrial capitalists. Ricardo suggested that as the population increased, land would become increasingly scarce and therefore increasingly valuable, so landowners would charge ever more for its use. More and more wealth would flow into the pockets of the landowners.

Karl Marx saw things slightly differently. By the time he was writing, in the mid-19th century, the appalling conditions of the urban poor were everywhere apparent. Land was no longer the focus of attention. Instead, Marx saw the horrific exploitation of children and older factory workers, working long hours in dangerous conditions, living in extreme poverty, while the factory owners were endlessly enriched. He predicted a path of relentless accumulation of capital by the factory owners that would only end when the desperation of the proletariat (the common people) led them to rebel. The communist and socialist movements were born at this time.

> '*The development of Modern Industry, therefore, cuts from under its feet the very foundation on which the bourgeoisie produces and appropriates products. What the bourgeoisie produces, above all, are its own gravediggers. Its fall and the victory of the proletariat are equally inevitable.*'
> Karl Marx, *Communist Manifesto* (1848)

Let it be

The opposite view to Ricardo's and Marx's apocalyptic view was that the market would work itself out, given time. This takes the principle of equilibrium and trusts that it will be attained if the market is given the chance to find its own level. Adam Smith's 'invisible hand' directing the market would, in this scenario, lead everything to turn out well in the end.

There are a couple of problems with this, not the least of which is that it can be inhumane. If it takes 50 years for the market to find its level, millions of people will endure lives of misery and abject poverty while waiting for it to happen. Another is that it's an untested theory – we have to gamble the welfare of the whole world to see if it's correct.

Seeing patterns

Economics today is based on statistics, in data that have been collected and processed rigorously. But such information has only been available for a relatively short while. The USA did not introduce income tax (and so have tax returns that show the level of income of the populace) until 1913, so US economists have only a hundred years' worth of data to work with. In 1955, the American economist Simon Kuznets produced a graph from the data (50 years' worth at that point) that reassuringly showed a bell-shaped curve for inequality. Inequality began at a relatively low level in 1910, then rose to a high point in the 1920s, and fell again in the 1950s. On the basis of this, he proposed that extreme inequality is a stage a growing economy will go through before settling to a sustainable level of equality.

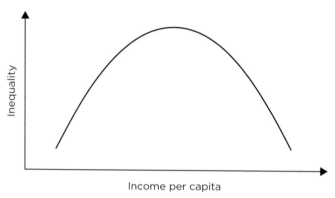

But the American economy did not come to an end in 1955. Whether inequality follows a bell-shape, ending with a low level, or a U-shape, ending with a high level, depends on which chunk of curve you look at.

Of course, 2015 is not the end of economic history either, so we still don't know which way it will go next. American economist Thomas Piketty suggests Kuznets' model was completely wrong, distorted by the impact of the two world wars and the intervening depression.

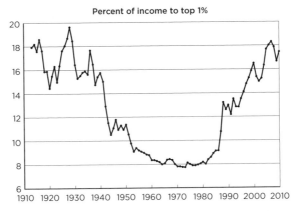

Percent of income to top 1%

Today, economists remain divided as to whether wealth inequality is destructive to economies as well as to the individuals who fall the wrong side of the curve.

The rich get richer . . .

Several economists suggest that the trend towards the rich accumulating more wealth and the poor becoming poorer is set to continue. The Canadian economist Miles Corak has found that as income inequality increases, social mobility falls. Alan B. Krueger, the chairman

> '**What drags down our entire economy is when there is an ultra-wide chasm between the ultra-wealthy and everyone else.**'
> US President Barack Obama (2012)

of the White House Council of Economic Advisers, has called this phenomenon the 'Great Gatsby Curve'. The result is that it is increasingly difficult for the poor to break out of their position of poverty – the 'American Dream' of the self-made individual rising through the ranks through merit and hard work is

> '*Equality of opportunity as we have known it no longer exists; we are steering a steady course toward economic oligarchy, if we are not there already.*'
> Franklin D. Roosevelt (1932)

becoming more and more difficult to realize.

One reason for this is the rise of so-called crony capitalism, which favours the individuals who currently have wealth and power, rather than favouring the market system itself.

In 2008, a cash injection of $700 billion (£453 billion) rescued Wall Street (the New York stock exchange) from the worst consequences of the economic crash. Analysing the outcome, economists

Emmanuel Saez and Thomas Piketty found that 93 per cent of the income gains from the 2009–10 recovery went to the top 1 per cent of taxpayers, and 37 per cent went to the top 0.01 per cent – an average of $4.2 million (£2.7m) per wealthy household.

'Most lobbying is pro-business, in the sense that it promotes the interests of existing businesses, not pro-market in the sense of fostering truly free and open competition.'
Luigi Zingales, University of Chicago Booth School of Business

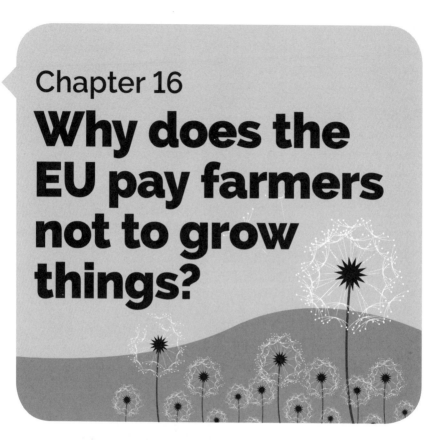

Chapter 16
Why does the EU pay farmers not to grow things?

The EU (European Union) pays 'set-aside' grants to farmers to leave fields empty.

The EU has many regulations and policies to help to protect traders within member states, but the oddest sounding are the grants paid to farmers *not* to grow crops or keep livestock.

A protective CAP

The Common Agricultural Policy (CAP) was introduced in 1958 to improve efficiency in agriculture in countries of the European Economic Community (or EEC, as the EU was then known). It was intended to benefit farmers, by guaranteeing them a fair price for their produce, and to benefit consumers, by producing higher quantities of better-quality produce. There were five aims. These were to:

- increase the productivity of agriculture
- ensure a fair standard of living for farmers
- stabilize the market for agricultural produce
- guarantee the food supply
- ensure fair prices for consumers.

The policy guaranteed a minimum price to farmers for their produce, no matter how much they produced. Farmers could choose to sell on the open market (where they might be able to get more than the minimum price) or sell to the EEC. The EEC promised to buy any amount of produce at the guaranteed minimum price so farmers did not have to worry if trading conditions in the open market were difficult. They could work out their budget based on the price set by the EEC.

In theory, if there was a glut of produce one year, the EEC would buy it and store it until there was a shortage, then sell it, protecting consumers from higher prices in those times. But the high guaranteed price led to farmers overproducing, because they had a guaranteed market for their produce no matter how much they grew.

Butter mountains and milk lakes

Surplus production led to 'lakes' of unsold milk and 'mountains' of surplus butter. The EEC was obliged to buy up surplus stocks at the agreed price, but that left it with food that was difficult to dispose of. There are few options. It can be:

- thrown away or destroyed
- fed to farm animals
- given or sold cheaply to countries outside the EEC.

Destroying food is unpopular, especially when there are people going hungry. In fact, much food was sold very cheaply to the USSR and developing economies. Some surplus stock was sold back to EEC farmers to feed to livestock. All these measures caused resentment among EEC consumers, who were paying high prices in the shops for food which they had already subsidised through taxes paid to the EEC. The taxes were used firstly to subsidise farmers and secondly to buy up the surplus food.

Even for the countries that received the cheap or free food, the system had its drawbacks. While food aid is helpful in times of urgent need, such as drought or crop disease, it can be more damaging than beneficial in the long term. The farmers in countries which receive cheap food cannot compete on price, so find it much harder to sell their own produce. They may be driven out of business, adding to those in poverty and leaving food insecurity when the supply of cheap or free food from overseas dries up.

Enough is enough

In 1984, a quota system was introduced to limit the amount of milk produced. Each EEC country was allocated a milk quota, which was divided between dairy farmers. Farmers could sell their quota on to others if they did not want to produce that much milk. Quotas provide a cheap way of controlling prices as there is no need to pay subsidies: the limited supply keeps prices high enough.

The EEC also imposed import restrictions in the form of tariffs (taxes). These artificially raise the price of agricultural products from overseas, so are unpopular with farmers elsewhere in the world. The duty on New Zealand lamb, for instance, protects European lamb farmers from cheaper competition.

More or less control

Some EU member states, including the UK, are considering leaving the EU and entering into their own, much freer trade agreement. They argue that the disadvantages of being tied to such a tightly controlling organization outweigh the benefits.

All nations face the same problem of striking a balance between encouraging free trade with other nations to boost their export markets, and discouraging cheap imports, which can put home producers at a disadvantage. The US, for example, has trade agreements with 20 nations (mainly Canada and those of Latin and South America). It is also negotiating regional trade agreements with the EU (Transatlantic Trade and Investment Partnership) and the Asian and Pacific countries (Trans-Pacific Partnership).

Paid to do nothing

In 1992, the EU introduced set-aside grants. These pay arable farmers to leave land uncultivated to prevent overproduction. If all the crops that could be grown were grown, either market prices would be too low to assure farmers of a good level of income, or the EU would have to buy up and dispose of surplus crops. It's easier not to have to deal with the produce in the first place, and this is achieved by

ECONOMIES OF SCALE

It usually costs less per item to manufacture a larger number of items than a small number. The bulk of the costs of production are the set-up costs (buying and installing machinery, for example), which must be paid no matter how many items are produced, and supplies (such as the raw materials), which are usually cheaper when bought in bulk. These 'fixed costs' become cheaper if they can be shared among a larger number of items. This is known as **economies of scale**.

Suppose a business wanted to print T-shirts. It might pay $400 to a designer for an original design, and $100 to a printing firm to set up its equipment to print the design. If it buys 100 plain T-shirts for $10 each, the total cost will be $1,000 + $100 + $400 = $1,500. The cost per T-shirt is therefore £15 and so must be sold at more than this price – $17, say – to make a profit.

However, if the business produced 1,000 printed T-shirts, the cost would be $10,000 + $100 + $400 = $10,500, or $10.50 per T-shirt. It would probably be able to buy plain T-shirts more cheaply because it had placed a larger order with the supplier. Perhaps the T-shirts now cost $8 each to buy. The total cost will then be $8,000 + $100 + $400 = $8,500, or $8.50 per T-shirt. The firm printing 1,000 T-shirts can then afford to sell them more cheaply – $12, say – than a firm printing 100 T-shirts, thereby undercutting its rival, and yet it would more than double its profit.

paying farmers not to grow it but to leave the land uncultivated (known as 'set-aside'). Farmers have to rotate the unused land, so as to avoid leaving the same areas uncultivated year after year.

Taking the CAP off

Removing the protection of the CAP would force many small farmers out of business. These farmers can't benefit from the economies of scale that large farms enjoy. Some have relatively poor land – Welsh hill farms, for example – and without subsidies could not survive. A free-market approach would say that these farms should be allowed to fail, but this would be both politically unpopular and perhaps foolhardy in the long-term. A secure food supply within the EU is an important security measure. If the EU is unable to provide food for its members in some possible future war or natural disaster, the region will

then be forced to buy produce on the open market and possibly pay cripplingly high prices.

Removing the subsidies to farmers and lifting import restrictions would save a lot of EU money. Some economists suggest this would not affect the profitability of successful farms, and consumers would be better off as prices would fall. Although farmers who stayed in business would receive less for their produce with the subsidy removed, it is argued that the price of farmland would fall as it would become a less attractive prospect. Small, unproductive farms would leave the market. The capital and labour deployed in these unprofitable farms could be used – with the aid of subsidies – to diversify into something more

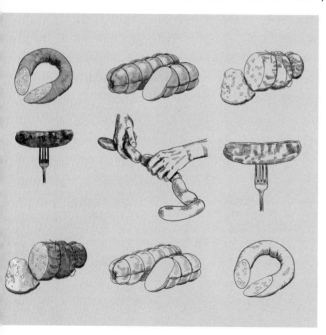

lucrative, such as regional crafts or food products (cheeses, pies, smoked meats, sausages and cakes for example), known as 'value-added products'. This doesn't take account of the human cost to the farmers who had lost their farms or farm workers who were unable to find jobs in the new economies.

Countries that benefit most from the CAP, in terms of receiving the largest amount in subsidies, are strongly in favour of keeping the current system and against any reduction in subsidies. This includes France, where farming makes up a large proportion of the rural economy and where farmers and farm workers consequently represent a powerful lobbying group. Other countries argue that they are being unfairly penalized by having to pay into a scheme from which they get little back, and which disadvantages their consumers by keeping prices artificially high.

Other CAPs

Subsidies are not only a feature of European agricultural policy. The USA and Canada also subsidise farmers, though not to the same degree. Subsidies account for around 15 per cent of farmers' income in the USA and 20 per cent in Canada. In the EU, subsidies are around 30 per cent of farm incomes, but elsewhere the proportion is even higher. In Japan, for example, it is over 50 per cent and in Switzerland (not part of the EU) it is close to 70 per cent.

Chapter 17

Is cash on the way out?

Cash has been around a long time in one form or another.

'Hard cash' represents an ever-decreasing part of the economy, as electronic forms of fund transfer take over. Yet despite this, the amount of cash in circulation is growing. Between 2008 and 2013, the value of British sterling bank notes in use increased by 29 per cent, and the value of euros in circulation

by 34 per cent. Between 2007 and 2012, the value of US dollars in circulation increased by 42 per cent. With the advent of cashless cards, the increased use of credit and debit cards and the steady increase in purchases online, are the days of cash numbered? And would it matter if they were?

A brief history of cash

Bartering – or exchanging – goods is a problematic form of trade (see page 20 – *What is money anyway?*) as it depends on the two parties wanting comparable items at the same time in order to make a satisfactory exchange. For example, a farmer may have piglets that he is anxious to sell before they begin to cost him money to feed, but he may wish in return to have some bags of wheat that have not yet been harvested. Around 8,000 years ago, the people of ancient Sumer, Babylonia and Mesopotamia began to develop a system of clay tokens to resolve this problem. The agreed exchange was written on clay tablets called 'bulla' on which the 'price' (two bags of wheat, in this example) was marked. Both sides in the transaction would keep one half of the tablet and the piglets (in this case) would be handed over. Once the wheat was harvested, the pig farmer would hand his half of the clay token to the wheat farmer and receive his promised two bags of wheat in exchange. In time, these clay tablets became tradable in themselves (see box).

In Ancient China, cowrie shells were used as tokens of trade. Around 1000BC the Chinese switched from using real shells to metal replicas as their pseudo-currency. In 800BC they began to adopt 'spade' and 'knife' money – tiny replicas of tools that came in different weights representing different values.

A PROMISE TO PAY THE BEARER

In ancient Mesopotamia, clay tablets inscribed in cuneiform with records of the deposit of commodities in state and temple warehouses were used as records of exchange and then as a form of 'promissory note'. A record of stored grain could be used to buy something else, the new recipient then being able to take the tablet and reclaim the deposited goods. The earliest surviving legal code, the Babylonian code of Hammurabi from 1760BC, regulates the use and trade of these contracts.

The Chinese were the first to devise paper banknotes, under Emperor Hien Tsung (AD806–21), but they missed out on the first coins – those were most likely produced in Asia Minor around 640BC and made of a silver-gold alloy called electrum. Other parts of the Greek-speaking world soon adopted the idea.

The invention of banknotes came about because there was a shortage of copper needed to mint coins. But the flirtation with paper notes was relatively brief: the ease with which they could be created meant the authorities gave in to the temptation to print money whenever they needed it, and runaway inflation resulted. As a consequence, the Chinese stopped making banknotes for many centuries.

Paper money didn't fare much better in Europe initially. The first

European bank notes were issued in Sweden in 1661 by the Stockholm banker Johan Palmstruch, who had the approval of the Swedish government. He, too, soon got carried away and printed more money than he could redeem from his deposits of silver.

He was prosecuted for fraud in 1668 and sentenced to death (though the sentence was later commuted to imprisonment).

As good as gold?

This poor track record couldn't stop the march of progress, though. It became impossible for precious metals alone to fulfil the demands for cash, so the first national banks sprang up and began issuing promissory notes that were more reliable than those of Palmstruch. Even so, the danger of inflation remained. It was largely kept in check by the 'gold standard'. This tied each nation's currency to the price of gold, which was set independently. Effectively, it meant there was a fixed exchange rate. In the USA, from 1834 to 1933, the price of gold was at $20.67 per ounce, while in the UK it was £3 17s 10½d. This meant £1 was worth $4.867. It worked as long as no participating country decided to massively overprint money.

The gold standard broke down around World War I, when nations printed extra money to finance their war efforts. It was reinstated after the war. Britain left the gold standard in 1931, during an economic downturn when a run on sterling made it impossible to maintain the price of the pound without depleting the country's gold reserves. This allowed the pound to be devalued and the British economy to recover. The gold standard eventually collapsed in 1971 when the US withdrew their promise to redeem overseas dollar-holdings in gold at $35 (£22.50) an ounce (part of the Bretton Woods system of 1944, see page 276).

Going . . .

We could argue that the heyday of cash ended with the emergence of cheques. But it's hard to say when they emerged. The Romans used something similar, called *praescriptiones*, in the first century BC, and 9th century Arabs and medieval Europeans used similar bills of exchange, but they didn't threaten cash.

POUND FOR POUND

The British 'pound sterling' is the oldest established currency still in use. The pound has existed since 1560, when Elizabeth I set its value at one troy pound (about 373 grams) of silver. The term 'sterling' first appeared in 1078 and denoted the purest form of silver available (around 99 per cent pure, also known as 'fine silver').

The earliest surviving modern-style cheque is handwritten and dates from 1659. The Bank of England was the first to issue pre-printed forms for writing cheques, introducing them in 1717. The

real boom in cheque use, though, came after 1959 when a machine-readable character-set made it possible to process large numbers of cheques automatically. With the advent of cheque guarantee cards in 1969, retailers were assured that cheques would be honoured, even if the account holder did not have the funds. (The bank took responsibility to reclaim the money from the account holder.) The surge in the use of cheques peaked in the 1980s and 1990s in most countries, when they became the next most popular method of payment after good old cash. Although billions of cheques were processed each year, cash still held its own.

. . . going . . .

Credit and debit cards were the next step. Banks phased out cheque guarantee cards from the mid-1990s, replacing them with debit cards. Customers still had to sign their name for each transaction, just as with a cheque. Debit and credit cards were then fitted with an electronic microchip on which was stored a personal identification number (or PIN). This system was called chip and PIN. These were considered more secure as they needed no signature (which could be forged) and the PIN was known only to the cardholder, so they gained ground rapidly. The trend towards online purchases, electronic bank transfers and secure online payment options such as Paypal also knocked a huge dent in the use of cash.

Now, instead of paying in a physical shop with cash, increasingly people were paying online by card or Paypal for goods that could come from anywhere in the world, with no need for buyers and sellers to convert between currencies. Even in the real world, debit and credit cards can be used internationally, so travellers have less need to carry foreign currencies.

... gone?

The use of contactless payment cards and mobile phone or other handheld devices to make purchases means there is still less need to carry cash today – even to buy small-value items. A few statistics show how the use of cash has declined:

- The value of payments made using cash has been well below the value of cashless payments for a long time: credit and debit card sales overtook cash in the UK in 2003.

- In 2015, the value of debit and credit card consumer sales was three times the value of cash sales.
- Early in March 2015, the number of transactions carried out in the UK using cash fell below the number using cashless payment methods for the first time.

- If we include all transactions, including those between large organizations and banks, the value of cash transactions in the UK in 2014 was £260 billion ($400bn). But the value of automated transactions was £76,643 billion ($118bn) – nearly 30 times as much.

Filthy lucre

Why don't we like cash? It's heavy, it's insecure (it can be lost or stolen), it takes more effort to count out and check cash than to wave a card, and it's dirty – a nice, clean card that has only ever been in your own possession seems so much more hygienic.

Most people have heard the urban legend that banknotes are contaminated with cocaine. A study in 1994 by the 9th Circuit Court of Appeals in Los Angeles, USA, found that three out of four bank notes were contaminated with cocaine or other illicit drugs. There have been similar findings elsewhere; a UK-wide study found a contamination rate of 80 per cent and in London in 1999 it was even worse – only four out of 500 banknotes tested were cocaine-free. During the SARS epidemic of 2003, China took the precaution of quarantining banknotes – those that were paid into banks were held for 24 hours before being released again, as the virus does not survive long outside a living cell.

> ### FALLING APART
>
> Germany had a problem with the literal disintegration of its currency when some euro notes started to crumble after being taken from ATMs. It transpired that the notes were contaminated with crystal meth from Eastern Europe, which contains a high level of sulphates; these mixed with sweat from people handling the notes to produce sulphuric acid, and this broke down the fabric of the notes.
>
> That doesn't happen to debit cards.

Last to go

People still use cash for shopping, but in ever decreasing numbers. Parking meters, vending machines and other mechanical payment devices are increasingly being converted to accept payment by phone or card. Buses and other forms of public transport still accept cash in many places (though London's buses have been cash-free since 2014), but contactless payment cards are becoming more common. The days of the cash-based vending machine are probably numbered too, as coins and notes are expensive to collect and bank. Currently, independent traders such as corner shop owners, newsagents and most market and street vendors still prefer to deal in cash because of the high cost of the levy imposed by credit card companies and banks. And then there is the underworld: traders who demand cash payments to avoid tax liability, for example. Drug dealers, prostitutes and hired assassins probably still deal in cash, too.

One of the great advantages of cash is that it's anonymous. But the diminished use of cash also makes it look a little suspicious – paying for an expensive object with cash raises eyebrows. In a bizarre twist of history, it seems that carrying cash – once the mark of wealth – is now a sign of being on the margins of society, and possibly even quite poor. In Sweden (which has gone furthest

TOP CASH-POOR COUNTRIES

Sweden leads the way, with only 3 per cent of transactions carried out in cash, but Somaliland (an autonomous region of Somalia) is not far behind. Purchases with mobile phones are more common there than almost anywhere else in the world, with even street vendors taking payment by phone. In Kenya, the M-pesa mobile money system has 15 million users. It's used not just for small payments, but for salaries, school fees and routine bills.

Canada decided to stop printing currency from 2012, using plastic bills instead (though they are still cash). Most Canadians (56 per cent) would sooner use an electronic wallet than cash anyway.

Experts predict the first totally cashless country will appear by 2030, if not before.

towards a cash-free economy), the number of bank robberies fell dramatically as electronic payment methods took over – from 110 in 2008 to just 16 three years later. Most Swedish banks simply don't handle cash any more. This trend is being adopted in UK and European banks, as indicated by the removal of security screens, which are not considered necessary as cashiers no longer handle large amounts of cash.

Is it worth it?

Cash is expensive. It costs a lot to manufacture and distribute; shops have to pay for secure storage and secure movement to the bank where it is deposited; handling and moving cash takes time; and counterfeit money is a burden on those who innocently accept it. A study in 2015 found that if the USA abandoned cash, GDP would increase by 0.47 per cent. It doesn't sound much in itself, but as GDP for the year was predicted to be $17.710 trillion (£11.5 trillion), that 0.47 per cent represents $83.237 billion (£54bn).

The cost of cash is highest for consumers in countries such as Denmark and Switzerland that have negative interest rates (as of 2015). This means that depositors have to pay just to keep their money in the bank. In Denmark, an interest rate for depositors of -0.75 per cent means it really is more prudent to keep their cash under the mattress.

Chapter 18

How do economic crashes happen?

The fragility of the world's money markets became painfully apparent in 2008.

In 2008, the good times came to an end for many of the world's economies. The flourishing economic growth seen over the previous decade was at an almost steroid-fuelled pace – and just as inadvisable as overdosing on steroids. The failure of the IndyMac Bank in the USA was the first sign that things were going horribly wrong in the financial markets. More banks and financial institutions followed IndyMac into collapse and the effect of this spread quickly around the world. The impact on businesses and individuals soon became catastrophic. Although governments bailed out some major banks to prevent a complete collapse of the banking system, the crash led to a worldwide recession worse than any since the Great Depression of the 1930s.

Money for nothing

Economists argue over the exact mix of the complex and interrelated causes of this crash, but there is general agreement that greed, over-confidence and too little regulation in the financial sector allowed a vast and precarious market to build on very insecure foundations. The value of the financial markets was, in fact, many times larger than the value of the real goods and services underlying it.

The trouble began with housing, and a decline in real estate values in the USA in 2007. But before that, the scene for disaster was set by banks creating too much extra money through making loans incautiously. Each time a bank lends money, it essentially creates money from nowhere (see page 125). In the years 2000–7, the amount of money and debt in the UK economy doubled, but only 8 per cent of the 'new'

money went into industries outside the financial sector. Around 31 per cent went into residential property and a further 20 per cent into commercial property; some 32 per cent went into the financial markets, and 8 per cent went to personal loans and credit cards. Other economies followed a similar pattern.

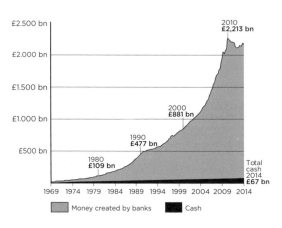

£2.500 bn
£2.000 bn
£1.500 bn
£1.000 bn
£500 bn

2010
£2,213 bn

2000
£881 bn

1990
£477 bn

1980
£109 bn

Total cash 2014
£67 bn

1969 1974 1979 1984 1989 1994 1999 2004 2009 2014

■ Money created by banks   ■ Cash

Subprime mortgages

In the past, if a potential house buyer wanted to take out a mortgage, a lender would assess the value of the house, the income of the applicant and their ability to pay the mortgage instalments. If the applicant's salary was too low, meaning that they might struggle to keep up the repayments, or if they had a bad credit record, so might default, or if the house seemed overpriced and might

decline in value over time, the loan was refused. This made financial sense.

As housing was in demand, the price for real estate was steadily climbing. Financiers could not see a reason why the trend would not continue. This made lending to buy housing – even risky lending – look attractive. Some American banks began offering high-risk loans – lending money to people with a higher-than-average chance of defaulting. These became known as 'subprime' mortgages. It was assumed that their houses would always increase in price, so if the client defaulted the house could be repossessed and sold to cover the outstanding loan. It seemed like a foolproof method of generating extra income for the banks at little additional risk.

Spreading eggs between baskets

Thinking that risky debts would be less risky if bundled together, banks pooled the subprime mortgages. The theory was that even if real-estate values fell in one region of the USA, they would not do so in other areas. By bundling loans from around the nation, risk would be spread and local fluctuations in the market would make little difference.

The pooled mortgages were used to back securities called Collateralized Debt Obligations (CDOs). They were divided into tranches based on assessed risk. This meant that all the least-likely-to-default mortgages were bundled together, all the most-likely-to-default were bundled together, and there were plenty of other bundles in between. Those considered most secure were given a triple-A rating, indicating that they were a safe bet. The rating was given by previously respected and trusted agents who were in the pay of the banks that created the CDOs. Unsurprisingly, they were overgenerous with their assessment of security.

The market for those baskets

Because interest rates were low, investors were keen to find options that paid a higher-than-average rate. The CDOs were that option. The risk was well-hidden, within the pooling and tranching, and the final product seemed very far removed from the struggling individuals who in earlier years would not have been given a mortgage in the first place. But they, in their insecure homes, were what the whole edifice was built on.

The CDOs were such an attractive proposition that many investors **leveraged** money to buy them – borrowing at a low interest rate to make an investment at a higher interest rate with the expectation of profiting from the difference in rates (see box). The problem is that if the investment doesn't pay off, the loan must still be repaid. The CDOs were traded between institutions in the US and also internationally.

The baskets break

ECONOMICS-SPEAK: LEVERAGING (ALSO 'GEARING')

Leverage is a technique used to maximize profits or losses. Typically, it involves gambling with interest rates or the values and future values of products or commodities. A person putting down a deposit on a house and taking out a mortgage to fund the rest of the purchase is leveraging their savings – they gamble on the assumption that the value of the house will rise over time, so they will end up with more, rather than less, equity in the house.

When American property prices fell, the system of CDOs collapsed. Instead of the decline in property values happening sporadically in different regions, it happened everywhere. The fragile subprime mortgages fell victim to the downturn as borrowers defaulted. Neither the home-owners nor the banks could sell the houses for enough to cover the value of the loan. As house prices fell, there was a massive problem with **negative equity** – the value of the homes was less than the mortgages taken out by the owners to buy them. Negative equity only becomes a problem when the owner needs to sell, but then it is a very big problem because the owner still owes money to the bank on a house he or she has already sold. High-risk borrowers who could not meet repayments defaulted on their mortgages because they could not simply sell and move. The banks that had loaned the mortgages stood to lose money and that meant

the CDOs lost value. No matter that the CDOs had been pooled and tranched – they were not as safe as the banks had claimed they would be and soon they were worthless. When they changed hands at all, they sold for rock-bottom prices.

The banks, forced by regulations to re-value their assets regularly at current prices, saw their capital value fall. This happened even though most of the borrowers at the bottom of the chain (the mortgage holders) might not actually default. The market was based on the assumption that they wouldn't, and the value of that assumption had fallen. It was, in effect, a market built on nothing.

Liquidity crisis

The collapse of subprime mortgages led to a **liquidity crisis**. Financial institutions struggled to convert the assets they held in the form of loans (and, increasingly, repossessed houses) into cash. The houses on which people had defaulted were often worth less, after their fall in value, than the money originally loaned to buy them. Even if the banks managed to sell the houses in an increasingly depressed market, they would still not recover all the money outstanding.

Another weak link in the chain was **credit-default swaps**. These are insurance policies taken out to guard against borrowers defaulting on repayments. So if you loaned a friend $1,000, you might take out insurance to cover him or her not paying you back. If your friend defaulted, the insurance would pay out. If they did not default, the insurer would keep the money you had paid. As soon as the chain started to break, insurers and banks that were insuring the loans crumbled under the burden of payouts. Just days after the bank Lehman Brothers declared bankruptcy (see box), the insurance company AIG also collapsed, brought down by the mass of credit-default risk it had insured.

The collapse of Lehman Brothers was a disaster not only for its employees and investors, but also for the wider economy. With the realization that even the biggest banks might be allowed to go under, all financial institutions panicked and stopped lending money. Without access to loans, even those businesses that had managed their finances responsibly found themselves in difficulty. They might simply have wanted to borrow money as part of a managed plan for expansion, or in the short term as part of an established operating

THE DEMISE OF LEHMAN BROTHERS

The US bank Lehman Brothers was the first major institution to become a casualty of the financial crisis. By 2007, Lehman Brothers was leveraged to a ratio of 31:1 (assets:owners' equity) meaning that it actually owned less than a thirtieth of its apparent assets and the remainder was based on borrowing. In particular, Lehman Brothers was overexposed in the subprime mortgage market. It had leveraged its capital to such an extent that even a slight downturn in the value of its assets (just 3–4 per cent) was enough to wipe out its entire value and led to its collapse in 2008.

pattern, but the banks were no longer willing to lend even to safe creditors. The effect snowballed, businesses slowed down or were unable to borrow to fund day-to-day transactions, and began laying off workers. As unemployment grew, people were buying less, manufacturing declined even further and more people were laid off. More banks suffered, more businesses suffered, more individuals suffered, and so the recession unfolded.

Although banks lacked the confidence or funds to lend to borrowers, they still expected the businesses and individuals they had already financed to pay back the loans and interest they owed. Just as a bank making a loan creates money, repaying a loan destroys money. So as loans were repaid, money was being taken out of the economy.

Bailing out and clawing back

The major western governments were forced to bail out the large banks to prevent a catastrophic collapse of the economy. Governments deemed these banks to be 'too big to fail' so had to provide the money they needed, sometimes by nationalizing them (taking them into public ownership). To fund these measures, the governments themselves had to borrow money, for example, by issuing bonds, leading to huge national debts. In order to repay these debts, they made cuts in public funding, leading to a reduction in public services and welfare/benefit payments, which became known as 'austerity measures'.

> '*If you owe the bank $100, that's your problem. If you owe the bank $100 million, that's the bank's problem.*'
> J. Paul Getty, rephrasing an old saying

Who's to blame?

Clearly the banks and finance industry were at fault. They had taken on large amounts of debt to finance investment without being sure to have enough wiggle-room to absorb any losses or shifts in the market. Greed, complacency and misplaced trust were at the root of the problem.

But banks don't operate in a vacuum. Regulators and central banks should be keeping an eye on them and stopping excesses that can lead to disaster. Regulators did not heed warnings as early as 2005

HIGH PRICE OF BAIL-OUT

The sum used to bail out British banks in 2009 was the most ever spent by the UK government in such a way. Until then, the largest sum paid out had been in 1834 with the compensation paid to Britain's 46,000 slave owners, following the abolition of slavery. This represented 40 per cent of government spending that year and was equivalent to £16–17 billion ($24–26bn) today.

that a savings glut (financed largely by Asia and Europe) was producing very low interest rates. This fed the desire to seek out higher-risk, higher-yield investments. Most catastrophically, regulators in the USA did not step in to save Lehman Brothers.

> *'Your company is now bankrupt, our economy is in crisis, but you get to keep $480 million (£276 million). I have a very basic question for you, is this fair?'*
> US Congressman Henry Waxman to Richard Fuld, CEO of Lehman Brothers, at the Committee on Oversight and Government Reform

Economists are divided on how far they hold different parties responsible. Right-wing economists tend to blame the US government and the housing policy that encouraged subprime lending; left-wingers tend to blame the greed of the financial institutions and under-regulation. It matters not as a means of apportioning blame, but because knowing the cause might help avoid a future crash. Maybe one day hindsight will make it all clearer.

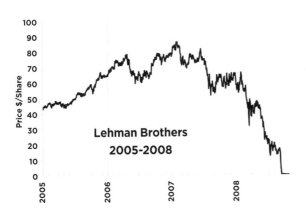

Lehman Brothers
2005-2008

Chapter 19

Does austerity work?

There are two possible and very different approaches to dealing with an economy in recession: spending or saving. In economists' terms, these are 'stimulus' or 'austerity'.

Starting with the problem

An economy in recession is sluggish, with little activity, often high debt and low spending. It is not economically productive, with very low growth, no growth or negative growth (meaning the economy is shrinking). There is no single official definition of recession, but a common requirement is two consecutive quarters (of a year) of falling GDP. Some economists cite a rise in unemployment of 1.5–2 per cent over a year as another sign of recession.

Recession can become not only a vicious circle but also a downward spiral. People don't spend money, so businesses make less money as demand falls. With less income from sales, businesses can't afford staff, so unemployment grows as demand for labour falls. People in jobs are nervous and those without jobs can't afford to buy as much, so spending falls again. This is called the **negative multiplier effect**. The further drop in demand prompts businesses to cut back more, and some businesses fail; further job losses means spending falls again. In a country with a welfare state that supports no- or low-income people, recession increases the need for benefits, so raises government spending.

At the same time, falling profits, rising unemployment or a reduction in spending and wages mean less is collected in taxes. The government has to pay out more in benefits, but is collecting less income, leading to a deficit. It might cut spending in other areas, such as road-building or defence, but that pushes those sectors into recession, too. If the government borrows money, it then has to pay it back, and pay interest on the loans. It can be hard to see a way out.

Spend, spend, spend

One way of tackling recession is for a government to stimulate the economy by injecting cash into it. For example, a government can increase public spending by building more roads and railway lines and by expanding education and healthcare. This employs labour and creates a demand for the goods and raw materials used. Although the government has to borrow or create money to do this, the money is going directly into the economy. Employment rises, people have the confidence to spend and the economy becomes more productive because of improved conditions. At first, people might remain anxious and save the extra money rather than spending it. Eventually spending goes up and more money goes into circulation, which leads to increased output from industry and a rise in jobs. Banks have the confidence to loan money to industry to fund expansion, and money comes into the economy to help fund the government's debt.

In time, the theory goes, people are earning and spending, so they are paying more in taxes and the government starts to recoup the money it has spent. As the economy picks up, the artificial stimulus is needed less and government spending can return to normal levels.

Belt-tightening time

An alternative to stimulus is austerity. In this case the government reduces spending and, as a consequence, many people in the country also reduce their spending. To save money, a government can cut welfare spending and spending on public goods and services. It can also limit public sector pay and pensions and reduce the interest paid on government securities. These measures have the immediate effect of reducing the amount the government has to pay out, but they also mean that many people have less to spend. The drop in spending can make the situation worse in the short term as the economy slows down further and the government income from taxes drops. The savings made by cutting public spending can then be used to fund a reduction in taxation on businesses and individuals in the private sector. The theory is that this will lead to an increase in general spending, as people have paid less in taxes and have more left over to spend. Businesses can then expand, employment increases and foreign trade expands. Money raised from cuts in one area of public spending can also be used to pay for growth in another, such as road and rail building and other areas of infrastructure. This also boosts employment

and increases spending and taxation. Obviously a government can only use the money it has saved in these ways – as a stimulus – if it does not already have large debts it has to finance and pay back. An economy in crisis, such as the Greek economy in the second decade of the 21st century, might resort to imposing strict austerity measures just to pay back debts, and with no intention or hope of funding public spending or tax cuts.

Austerity and war

Many economies imposed austerity programmes during the two world wars of the 20th century. In these cases, the government needed to raise (or save) money to fund an expensive war effort and to secure essential food and other services while a portion of the population was away fighting. After the USA entered World War I, it imposed a top income tax rate of 77 per cent in 1919. The government took control of the food supply and fixed the prices of staple foods and other essential items. Fuel use was banned on certain days, and daylight saving time introduced. But an economy during war is very different from an economy in recession. The US economy had been booming before the war, and popular

support for the war effort made for a different spirit among the population than the ground-down weariness of people who have faced long-term economic hardship.

When war came again in 1939, it actually helped to lift some economies out of recession or depression as it brought demand for goods and services and raised employment.

Lessons from history

The last major world recession, before the crash of 2008, happened in the 1930s and is called the Great Depression. It came about after the American stock market on Wall Street crashed spectacularly. The US called in overseas loans and imposed barriers to imports to protect American producers. The result was that the depression spread to other regions, particularly Europe.

By 1933, 13–15 million Americans (20 per cent of the population) were unemployed and nearly half the nation's banks had failed. The situation was disastrous. People were starving, queuing for food at soup kitchens. Many people lost their life savings, jobs or homes when the banks crashed, and some killed themselves in despair.

Farming had been in crisis in the USA for years, caused in part by the switch to inappropriate farming methods, which had led to severe drought. Tenant farmers could not pay back loans to banks, their farms were repossessed and farm workers laid off, leading to further unemployment and mass movement of workers between states. The USA had less welfare support than the UK and the situation for many people was desperate.

One approach

In Britain, the 'heavy' industries of ship-building, coal-mining and steel-smelting, mainly concentrated in Wales, northern England and Scotland, were the first to fail. In the town of Jarrow, every single adult male was unemployed. In the south, though, the newer 'light' industries were much less badly affected, leading to severe north–south inequality. The government increased taxes and cut unemployment benefits to try to reduce its own spending. It also imposed import duties, which were intended to protect British industry, but led to a further downturn in trade as other countries retaliated with their own import tariffs. These austerity measures possibly made matters worse.

At the same time, some government actions helped the situation. They increased the amount of money in circulation and reduced interest rates, encouraging people who had money to spend it. (There is little incentive to save if interest rates are low.) They used incentives to encourage industries to start up or move to depressed areas and provide employment. And they built 500,000 new homes, which not only provided much-needed housing but also provided jobs and demand for materials, which invigorated the economy. This is an example of cuts in one area of public spending being used to fund increased spending in another.

Another approach

The USA changed tack after a few years, beginning with austerity and switching to stimulus. The president at the start of the Depression was J. Edgar Hoover. He believed the recession would run its course and the economy would naturally recover. He tried to bail out some of the banks with government loans in the hope that the effect would 'trickle down' to working people. As a Republican, he firmly believed in a free-market economy and that government should not intervene in its workings. Hoover lost the presidential election to Democrat Franklin D. Roosevelt in 1932. By the time Roosevelt was inaugurated in 1933, all the banks were closed and the government did not have the money to pay its own employees.

'The only thing we have to fear is fear itself.'
Franklin D. Roosevelt, US president.

Roosevelt introduced emergency measures to stabilize the banks still considered sound and launched his 'New Deal', which provided jobs and stimulus through massive government projects such as building dams and hydroelectric power stations that would make other industries possible in depressed areas. Although recovery was not smooth, it was substantial. The end of World War II finally marked the end of the Depression.

What will work now?

Austerity and stimulus have been used in varying degrees by different nations to confront the economic crisis that began in 2008. Economists disagree about what, if anything, is working. The verdict of the International Monetary Fund (IMF) is that austerity doesn't work and that countries which have adopted predominantly austere measures have fared worse than those which have opted for stimulus – for spending their way out of recession. In 2013, the chief economist of the IMF, Olivier Blanchard, accused the UK government of 'playing with fire' by continuing to pursue austerity measures. In 2015, however, the managing director of the IMF, Christine Lagarde, said the UK authorities had managed to provide the right balance of spending cuts and revenue raising. '. . . when we look at the comparative growth rates delivered by various countries in Europe, it's obvious that what's happening in the UK has actually worked.' Only time will tell who was right.

Chapter 20

How long will the shops stay open?

Shops are closing; some very big names have closed their doors for the final time in the last decade or so. Some of the shops that have shut down had been around for a century or more. Does it matter that they are going?

One in nine working Americans works in retail. It used to be more – 1999 was the high point in shop working. Between 1950 and 1990, jobs in retail grew at a rate 50 per cent above general employment, but then the trend reversed and since 1990 jobs in retail have grown 50 per cent more slowly than other jobs. A similar pattern is seen elsewhere in the world. What has happened to the shops?

Late, great industries

Other industries have suffered similar declines in the past (see page 132 – *Don't we still have to make things?*). First agriculture and then manufacturing industries have been subject to falling labour as mechanization and efficiency have increased. At the start of the 20th century, more than 40 per cent of Americans worked in agriculture. Now the USA produces more food than a hundred years ago but with less than 2 per cent of the population working in farming. Manufacturing now employs about 10 per cent of Americans, compared with around 30 per cent ten years ago. It looks as though retailing might be the next sector of the economy that will face declining employment.

Window shopping and Windows shopping

One of the biggest changes has been the internet revolution, with the result that much of retail is carried out online. Online shopping gives us more choice, often lower prices, and saves a trip to the shops. One disadvantage of shopping online is the need

WHERE DO YOU WORK?

Top employment sectors in the USA (2013):

1 Retail trade
2 Accommodation and food services
3 Professional and technical services
4 Administrative and waste services
5 Education (local public elementary/primary and secondary schools)

to wait in for delivery, and even that problem is fast disappearing as more businesses offer a network of local collection points. By 2015, around 12 per cent of purchases in the UK were online, a quarter of these through Amazon, the United States' largest online retailer. Its rise has been meteoric, from 19 billion US sales in 2008 to over 61 billion sales four years later. Its founder, Jeff Bezos, has an estimated net worth of $33 billion (£21.4bn).

The profitable few

Amazon employs staff to pack and dispatch orders with an average annual salary of $24,000 (£15,000). But the average income that each full-time employee generated for Amazon was $600,000 (£390,000) in 2014 (down from over $1 million (£650,000) in 2011), three times the average sum a traditional retailer gains from a full-time employee.

Until recently, customers preferred to buy goods such as furniture, clothes and shoes in store where they could examine them firsthand. But there has been a growing trend for shoppers to browse in real shops and then order their chosen item more cheaply online. The growth in shopping comparison websites and smartphones has meant people can even do this from their phones while standing in the shop. To counter this trend, many shops now have their own websites offering goods more cheaply than in store, plus a click-and-collect service.

There is one bright spot, though. Shoppers are more likely to make impulse buys in a shop than online, with around a third of in-store purchases being spontaneous rather than planned.

The Walmart effect

Online shopping has not been the only blow to conventional retailing. The so-called 'Walmart effect' captures the impact of massive low-end retailers moving into

a local market. Walmart is a chain of discount department stores and retail warehouses based in the USA. When Walmart opens a store, it can save low-income families living in the area up to 30 per cent on their food bills, taking account not only of Walmart's low prices but also of the price reductions other stores are forced to make in order to compete. There are, inevitably, further consequences. A study in 2008 found that for every job created in a new Walmart store, 1.4 retail jobs are lost as other stores close or downsize.

Self-service and no service

Shopping had already undergone a major revolution in the 20th century with the introduction of self-service, initially in grocery stores. In the first half of the century, most shoppers were served personally by a shop assistant. The idea of touching goods unsupervised would have been unthinkable. Other customers waited patiently in line until a staff member became free, which limited the number of sales – especially in busy periods. Employing extra staff to cope with the busy periods meant they were not working – and not making money for the store – at other times.

This began to change with the introduction of 'self-service', pioneered by US entrepreneur Clarence Saunders, who opened his

first 'Piggly Wiggly' self-service grocery store in 1916. The concept soon spread throughout the US and beyond. Self-service increased sales dramatically as retail staff were needed only to take payment at the checkout and stock shelves. By 1951, the UK's Premier chain of self-service supermarkets was taking ten times as much in sales as equivalent traditional British grocery stores.

Now, nearly all shops are fully or partly self-service. The introduction of self-service checkouts and hand-held scanning devices has cut staff and therefore costs even further. The need to engage with technology might make it seem that there is little advantage over online shopping any more. The boundary between online and real-world shopping is certainly blurring, with the option to have online orders delivered to a nearby store for collection, to order online in a store if items are out of stock, and to compare prices by phone while standing in a shop.

Two markets

Increasingly, high street shopping has become polarized. There is the budget end of the market, where low price is everything, and the 'high-end' where quality, exclusivity and customer service have the most impact on purchasing decisions. The pure white, minimalist styling of the Apple Store is an example of this trend. The space is not used efficiently; only a handful of products are on sale, albeit in different colours and configurations. Accessories are placed discreetly against the walls, out of the way, leaving most of the floor space as a shrine to the elegant, stylish technology. The staff are attentive and knowledgeable. Customer service and image are on offer as much as the goods, which are relatively expensive.

At the other end of the scale are the discount stores, which prioritize low price and abundance of choice. This approach was pioneered in the UK by East-End trader Jack Cohen, founder of the

Tesco supermarket chain, whose slogan 'pile it high, sell it cheap' has been widely adopted by clothes shops such as Primark and general stores such as Poundland. Stores like these prioritize price and abundance of choice. Often the queues are long (because the shops are popular), and the shop floor noisy and crowded. But a peaceful shopping

experience is not what people are there for: they want cheap goods. Indeed, the noisy bustle, which creates something of the feel of a market, might even be part of the attraction.

How can stores like Primark afford to sell things so cheaply? For one thing, they manufacture in areas of the world where labour is cheap, but so do a lot of more expensive brands. They only sell their own branded goods, so there is no intermediary taking a share; they place huge bulk orders, so benefit from economies of scale (see page 208); their production processes are highly efficient; they use cheap raw materials; they don't run expensive advertising campaigns; their stores are basic and functional, making economic use of floor space. This is a total contrast to Apple Store.

The squeezed middle

In some areas of retailing, it is the middle-grade shops that are struggling; those that serve the now-struggling middle classes. High-end retailers catering to the wealthy have been largely unaffected by recent economic conditions as the income of the wealthiest consumers has not dropped. Discount and budget retailers have seen business increase as more middle-class shoppers have moved down-market as their incomes have dropped. In the middle, many of the stores that used to dominate the high streets and shopping malls are struggling.

Does it matter?

Who loses out if shops close? Most obviously the people who own and work in the shops. Retail is a very large employment sector, and people displaced from jobs in retail will seek new jobs with a similar skill set. Most retail jobs are relatively low-paid, low-skilled jobs. This type of job is considered by economists to be fungible – that is, workers are relatively easy to replace. The difficulty arises when there are not enough jobs to swap into. Online shopping is less labour intensive, so moving retailing online may lead to a fall in jobs in retail.

There is an impact on cityscapes, too, with shops falling empty. A domino effect also comes into play as closing shops and empty units mean fewer people are attracted into town centres and shopping malls. Reduced footfall leads to further shops closing, and so on.

The rise of the online retailer

While online shopping may have hit the traditional retail sector hard, it has also opened up new retail opportunities for those willing to take advantage of them. Many people now sell goods and services from home, through their own websites or through the giant online outlets such as Amazon and eBay. The start-up costs and annual overheads involved in working from home are minimal compared with those associated with opening and running a traditional shop. This reduces or eliminates the need to take out expensive loans – with the high risk of bankruptcy if the business fails – giving many more people the confidence to start a business. Online shopping has also provided work for (so jobs in) courier and delivery services.

GRIM OUTLOOK
According to the UK's Centre for Retail Research (CRR), while around 5 per cent of shops were empty in 2008, 14 per cent were vacant five years later. The centre predicts that around a quarter of shops in Britain will close by 2018.

Chapter 21

How does the stock market work?

The stock market is at the heart of national economics – we hear about it on the news, but what does it actually do?

The stock market allows people (and organizations, such as pension funds) to trade in little portions of companies. These portions – called stocks and shares – entitle the owner to have a say in how a company is run and/or claim a **dividend**. The dividend is a payout representing a portion of the company's profits.

Sharing a company

Imagine that you wanted to start a business, perhaps making giant kites. Certain costs would be incurred in setting it up, including:

- renting premises in which to conduct business
- sourcing materials and processes
- hiring and paying the workers
- marketing the kites
- distributing or delivering the kites
- running the business itself (administration, accounting, and so on)
- paying taxes and costs associated with the workers (such as pension contributions, health insurance and sick pay).

You could choose to start on a small scale and take on more staff as the orders grew, or you could choose to seek investment capital and start at a more ambitious scale. If you chose the second path, you might be able to borrow money from friends and family or from the bank, or you might look for outside investors who would give you money in exchange for a share in the company. Some types of business can only be started at quite a large scale with investment capital. If instead of making kites you wanted to make planes or start a telecoms network, you could probably not fund it from your own pocket, even with the help of family, and a bank would be unlikely to lend you all the money you needed.

An investor is not going to lend you money unless they think you will make a profit and so be able to pay them a return on their investment. They might also expect to have a say in how you run the company, as they won't want to see their money wasted through poor business decisions. To secure their claim on any profit and to have some input into how you run the business, they buy a share of it.

Stocks and shares

The total capital (assets) of a company that could be divided between the owners if the company went into liquidation is called its **stock**, or **capital stock**. A portion of a company sold to an investor is called a **share**. There are many different types of shares. One of the most important types is **common** or **ordinary shares**. These entitle the owner to have a say in how the company is run, to be paid a sum of money called a dividend – a proportion of the company's profits – each year, and to own a share of the assets. If a company starts with a stock-holding of 1,000 shares, someone who buys 100 shares will own 10 per cent of the company. They also have 10 per cent of the votes at shareholder meetings, where company policy and plans are discussed, they gain 10 per cent of the shared-out profits, and they have a claim to 10 per cent of the company's assets.

Another type of share, called a **preferred share**, has no voting rights but pays a higher dividend and has a preferential claim on assets. If the company were to fail and go into liquidation, the preferred shareholders would receive their share of the stock before ordinary shareholders. Together, the shareholders own the company.

More investment

Start-up is not the only point at which a company might need investment capital. If your kite-making business went well, you might want to move to larger premises or order new, better machinery. You could raise more money (capital stock) by selling more shares. The new shareholders would also have rights over the assets, rights to dividends, and perhaps votes in board meetings. Before new shares can be issued, the existing shareholders have to agree to the move, because it reduces the value of their own shares. They are often given first refusal – the right to buy the new shares before they are offered to anyone else. It might seem as though it would be unwise to allow more shares to be issued, but it is done with the intention of making the company more profitable, so everyone will benefit in the long run.

FROM POTATO SALADS TO THE GREEK ECONOMY

A new way of funding start-ups is **crowd-funding**. In this model, the aspiring business owner starts an online campaign to attract funding from many individuals, some offering only tiny amounts (as little as $10/£6.50). The investors don't typically own shares, but are given a specific one-off reward in exchange for their investment. If the fundraising campaign reaches its target, all the money is delivered to the entrepreneur who is then obliged to deliver the rewards and start the business. If the target is not met, none of the money is delivered (it is all returned to the would-be donors) and the entrepreneur has no responsibilities (and no money).

Crowd-funding can be more or less ambitious, cover any type of business venture, and be more or less serious in intention. As a joke, American Zach Brown started a campaign on Kickstarter to raise $10 £6.50) so that he could make a potato salad. In the end, he raised $55,000 (£35,000) and held a huge party at which a lot of potato salad was served. At the other extreme, Thom Feeney tried to crowd-source 1.6 billion euros (£1.2bn/$1.8bn) through Indiegogo to bail out the Greek government during its debt crisis in 2015. In just eight days it had raised nearly €2m (£1.5m/$2.2m) towards its huge target.

Private and public companies

Your kite-making business might very well start off as a private limited company. This means that its shares are not traded on the open market, but you can offer shares to people of your choice. Sale of shares can be restricted, so none of the shareholders can unilaterally sell their shares to just anyone. Although this limits the pool of available investors it means it's easier to keep control of the company.

Large corporations are often public limited companies (or public traded companies in the USA). Their shares are traded on the open market and listed in the appropriate stock market (depending on the country in which they are registered). Anyone can buy shares. This means that unless the original owners keep at least 51 per cent of the shareholding themselves, they can lose control of the company, as others can work together to vote against them in shareholder meetings. Shareholders direct the course a company takes. Sometimes, the founders of a company are dismissed by shareholders acting in unison against them.

Buying and selling

When shares are listed on the stock market, they can be traded openly, meaning they are bought and sold by stockbrokers and investors. The price for which shares in a company are sold is an indication of the financial health of the company. Suppose shares in your kite-making business originally sold for $10 each. The company gets off to a good start and at the end of the year the value of its capital (stock) has increased by 20 per cent. This means the value of each share has also increased by 20 per cent. Someone who wanted to sell their shares should be able to get $12 for each of them. That's a good return on an investment for a single year. Shares are a risky investment, though. If the business had done badly and lost value, perhaps

STEVE JOBS – IN AND OUT OF A JOB

Steve Jobs and Steve Wozniak founded Apple Computers in 1976, but needed to raise funds to promote their first serious computer, the Apple II. To do so, they sold shares the following year. They sold so many shares that they lost control of the company six years later. Investors felt Jobs was too young and inexperienced to run a large company and in 1983 John Sculley, previously boss of Pepsi, was appointed to run the company. Sculley and Jobs clashed frequently, and in 1985 Jobs left, starting a new computer company called NeXT. A series of executives then ran Apple, but were not sufficiently innovative or imaginative to reinvigorate the company once its original products began to show their age. Eventually, Apple bought up NeXT – and with it, Jobs – and from 2000 he ran Apple again, overseeing it as it rose from strength to strength and added new markets to its portfolio.

because of an economic downturn and a fall in sales, the shares would be worth less than the shareholder paid for them. For this reason shares should be regarded as a long-term investment. Provided the business is basically sound, short-term fluctuations in the price of shares can be ignored as, over time, the shares should increase in value. This is the traditional attitude towards buying and trading in shares, but the current stock market has many different types of investor, some with very short-term aims.

Round and round

The value of shares is affected not only by how well the company does in trading, but also by the price for which the shares change hands. This looks like a circular argument, and it is. If the company is seen to be doing well, people want to buy the shares – there is demand for them. Consequently, their price goes up further. If the company is doing badly, and people think it will continue to do badly, the share price falls. Nervous investors sell their shares. There is an oversupply of shares and little demand for them, so the price drops further.

At this point, when the share price is low, a speculator might come in and buy up a lot of shares for a low price. They do this if they think the company will recover, or if they can buy enough shares to influence the direction it takes and hope they can make it profitable again.

All blag and bluster

The stock market is extremely volatile. Share prices are affected not just by announcements of profit and loss but by other factors that might affect the market for the company's goods and services or its ability to sell them. A pharmaceutical manufacturer's shares will rise in value if it announces a new medicine to combat a common disease, for example. But if a medicine was withdrawn because of a safety scare, the share price would fall. It might fall, too, if a rival company launched a more successful product. The fall could come before the new product even reached the market – it's all about confidence and expectations. It is for this reason, as much as to appeal to customers, that businesses put so much effort into maintaining a good public image, and spend a great deal on public relations.

Sometimes a company can be destroyed by its poor performance on the stock exchange, even though it appears to be operating normally on a day-to-day basis. If its share value falls too far, banks will not allow an overdraft or loan, suppliers will not allow credit, and customers may be afraid that orders will not be fulfilled. The crisis of confidence can wreck a business.

Money for nothing

The investors in a company risk their capital (in the form of invested money) in the hope of a good return. The dividends they are paid and the increase in value in their shares is the reward they gain for the risk they take – the risk of losing their money. It is not the same as the reward workers receive, which is payment in return for their labour.

To the labouring worker, return on capital can look like money for nothing. A shareholder might hold stock for only a matter of weeks, days or even hours and sell it again to make a quick profit and earn more money than an employee makes in a whole year.

Successful traders in shares have a talent for speculating – for anticipating which shares will do well, and then buying and selling them at optimum moments. They have put time into learning about and following the stock market, but they are not adding anything to the value of the firm's products. Whether a company's share price goes up or down a little makes scant difference to the performance of its products in the marketplace. But a significant change in share price can make a difference to market performance, often without reflecting any genuine change in the value of the products.

The changing nature of speculation

Until the 1960s, most investors bought stock in order to get the dividends rather than to make a profit trading. Then people began speculating in the modern sense, buying and selling stock to make gains on the capital itself. It was argued that it was not really speculating, as the true value of stock is whatever you can sell it for. Financial institutions then began offering more and more varied – and obscure – financial products to investors.

The standard financial product is the **derivative**, a product whose value is based on (derived from) the value of the underlying asset. During the 1990s, financial products multiplied, bearing less and less relation to the real businesses at the base of the structure. Now the 'products' being traded were often far removed from the productive asset – the share in a hotel, publishing company or other business that sold a genuine service or good. Financial products proliferated to the point where they could no longer be supported in any meaningful way by the asset they were based on. Indeed, by 2007 world GDP was $65.6 trillion (£42.5 trillion), but the value of the financial asset market was $900 trillion (£583 trillion). The financial sector had become largely independent of the industries on which it was originally built.

Even though there seems to be little connection between derived financial goods and 'real' markets, speculation puts up the price of real goods and services. The World Bank estimated that in 2010, 44 million people worldwide were pushed into poverty because of high food prices caused, at least in part, by speculators pushing up the price of basic commodities.

> *'Unless policymakers understand that the financial industry isn't necessary for the real economy any more, and that it should scale down dramatically, the sector will remain a gigantic parasite on top of the real economy.'*
> Andy Xie, independent economist, formerly of the investment firm Morgan Stanley

The growing parasite

Financial markets have filled with more and more abstruse 'products' that have no bearing on real goods and services. They include, for example, buying and selling 'futures' (the promise to purchase goods at a fixed price at a future date) and reselling bundled insurance risks. Some economists, even previous financiers, are calling the financial industry parasitic.

Chapter 22

Does aid help or hinder?

Overseas aid is a contentious issue.

Some people question whether we should give aid to foreign countries at all when there are people at home who are in need. Then there is the broader question of whether aid actually helps, has no impact or might even make things worse for people in developing countries.

Setting goals

The United Nations has set a target for developed countries to spend 0.7 per cent of gross national income (GNI) on official development assistance (ODA) for less economically developed countries. In 2014, Denmark, Norway, Luxembourg and Sweden exceeded that target and the UK was on target; all other countries fell below it.

First and other aids

Aid can have short-term or long-term goals, be given by one country, or a group of countries acting together, or by individuals giving to charity. It can be given with or without conditions.

Emergency aid is given to alleviate the immediate effects of a sudden disaster such as an earthquake, flood or famine, through rescue work and emergency food, shelter and medication. It is often supplied by charitable giving, including donations made by individuals, and is handled by international aid agencies such as the

International Red Cross and Médicins Sans Frontières. Many national governments contribute to emergency aid financially and by providing food, medicines, equipment and specialist (often military) personnel.

Long-term development aid is given to raise standards of living in a country over time. This can follow on from emergency relief or be used to help a country that is impoverished by long-term environmental, social or political problems. It aims to improve education, healthcare, infrastructure and other fundamental services so that people and economies can become more productive in the long term.

One individual country giving to another is called **unilateral aid**. An international organization such as the United Nations giving to a country is called **multilateral aid**. The aid might be financial or in the form of supplies or expertise.

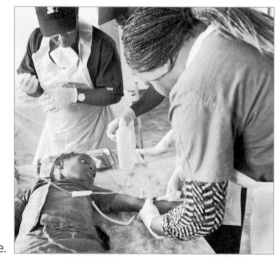

With and without strings

Aid given freely is called **grant aid**. More often, aid is **tied** or **conditional**, meaning that it comes with strings attached. This might be, for example, that funding for a development (like a dam or railroad) is given on condition that the contract to build it goes to a business based in the donor country. The recipient gets

the benefit of the infrastructure – the new dam or railway – and the money used to make it benefits the donor country through increased employment and tax revenue from the participating company. The project will usually employ local labour and might source materials locally, thereby putting extra money into the local economy. This form of aid can benefit communities in the short term, through increased local employment and trading opportunities, and in the long term by improving infrastructure. However, this is not straightforward, as it needs to be managed carefully or it can unbalance a local economy, putting up prices for the local community or even leading to shortages. The requirement to use an organization based in the donor country restricts choice in terms of pricing and exactly what is built and how it is built.

What is aid for?

The overall aim of aid is to raise living standards for the poorest people in the world, but to do this in ways that are sustainable. It is not just a matter of giving food to hungry people or tents to people whose homes have been destroyed in a hurricane (emergency relief), but involves helping to build fair economies in which no one is destitute and the community as a whole is economically productive. It's a tall order. The world's poorest communities struggle with some seemingly insuperable problems, including poor-quality land, hostile climate, scant natural resources, political turmoil, oppression and war. These are not conditions in which it is easy to build a thriving economy.

There is no magic wand that can transform a poor economy into a healthy one. But there are many long-term measures that can provide a community with a more hopeful future, including funding education, vaccination programmes, healthcare and essential infrastructure such as roads and a clean water supply. Funding (or loan of expertise) for these developments might not alleviate the short-term needs of the poorest people, but it should build better prospects for the future. Opinion amongst economists is divided as to how effective it is.

MILLENNIUM VILLAGES PROJECT

The Millennium Villages Project is an initiative started at the Earth Institute at Columbia University, USA, by economist Jeffrey Sachs to provide a sustainable aid programme to villages in Africa. It aims to address all aspects of community life at once, helping to develop education, healthcare, sustainable local industries and sustainable agriculture. People are helped to start businesses and build homes and latrines, with the emphasis being on helping them to help themselves so that the changes endure and perpetuate. The approach is very individual, with a budget of $110 (£71) per villager per year for five years. This usually provides: fertilizer and high-yield seeds, clean water, basic healthcare and education, mosquito bed nets, and a communication link to the outside world. Villages included in the scheme have seen increased agricultural productivity of up to 350 per cent. Sachs also promotes what he calls 'clinical economics'. This involves an individual diagnosis of a community's needs, and then designing an aid programme that is individually targeted to them. He has advised on aid to Russia, Poland and Bolivia – countries with very different needs.

Why give money away?

Support for foreign aid is far from universal. Many people argue that it is not our problem, and they would rather the money they pay in taxes is used in their own country, to benefit the home population directly. But there are economic and political reasons to help the

poor in developing countries – essentially, it *is* our problem.

Long-term development aid – if it works – should make the world better for all of us. Oxford economist Paul Collier has said that aid should be prompted first by compassion and second by 'enlightened self-interest'. The compassion we feel for less fortunate people prompts us to do something, and enlightened self-interest will keep us motivated once we get into the tedious nitty-gritty of sorting out an aid programme. Enlightened self-interest might manifest, for example, in recognizing that there will be fewer economic migrants if people can find work in their own country, or that a developing economy will later become a valuable customer base.

Global productivity

The whole world benefits when each country puts its resources to the best possible use, so raising global productivity. In addition, if the poor are desperate, and without hope, they might be more likely to join extremist organizations, support oppressive dictators (who can destabilize a region through military conflict), to farm opium poppies and to become refugees, asylum seekers and economic migrants. People with a sustainable living in their own country tend to stay where they are.

Top down and bottom up

There are two broad approaches to aid: 'top down' and 'bottom up'.

Top-down aid focuses on providing financial or other help to those in power within a country with the hope that it will be used or distributed to help the people most in need. This form of aid may come with restrictive conditions on how it may be used. Financial aid may be given in the form of a low-interest loan or debt relief (cancelling or reducing the interest on loans). Where aid is practical, including equipment, food or loan of expert staff, restrictions might be placed on exactly how it is to be used.

Bottom-up aid is largely administered by the donor and goes directly to the poorest people. An example would be the

International Red Cross distributing mosquito nets in Uganda. Because bottom-up aid does not work through the official distribution channels and networks within a country, it is often the only way of getting aid to people in war-torn and disaster-struck areas where transport infrastructure has been disrupted.

In general, larger sums are given as top-down aid, but there are also more restrictions on its use.

Does it work?

Whether or not aid programmes actually work in achieving their goals is a question that is debated by the world's top economists. Aid has come in for the following types of criticism – and this is not an exhaustive list:

- It enriches the ruling elite and criminal gangs in the recipient countries by being stolen, misdirected or otherwise diverted from its intended destination and never reaching those in most need

- It produces a culture of dependency rather than helping a community to develop a sustainable economy that will make them financially secure and independent
- It props up oppressive, undemocratic or corrupt regimes, preventing the society adopting a fairer form of government
- It can disrupt or destroy local markets by flooding the rural

WOMEN AT WORK

Studies by the international aid agency Oxfam have found that one of the most effective ways to use aid in developing countries is to set up independent, female-run farm collectives. Here plots of land are farmed individually or collectively by women with the produce being pooled and sold on the open market or through fair trade agreements. Money channelled through women in this way, rather than the male community or tribal leaders, has led to improved crop yields, higher market prices and a marked improvement in the economic prosperity of the community in general and their families – and especially the children – in particular.

economy with cheap or free goods that make local produce uneconomic to produce and sell

- It may be wrongly targeted or inappropriate – such as food that is not recognized or unacceptable on dietary or social grounds and so ends up wasted.

Making matters worse?

The American economist William Easterly has made many criticisms of top-down aid. In particular, he criticizes the effects of debt relief. Writing off debts, he suggests, does not release money for the poor – but benefits the wealthy ruling elite who usually spend it abroad, in economically developed countries, without even creating a trickle-down effect (see page 128). He argues, too, that debt relief encourages overspending (in order to secure relief) and might encourage further borrowing if rulers believe future debts will also be written off. It is also unfair to those countries that did pay back their loans.

He criticizes the aid culture that portrays helping African and other poor nations as a task initiated and achieved by richer governments and individuals. This denies or minimizes the role of poor countries in helping themselves. He prefers an approach he calls 'free development' that puts the needs, rights and desires of people in a developing country first, with them helping themselves out of poverty and solving their own problems.

BUILDING SCHOOLS – AN OLD-SCHOOL APPROACH?

Some of the traditional types of aid activity, such as building schools to encourage education, are currently under scrutiny. The lack of school buildings is not always the root cause of low education: it can be down to children not attending existing schools, or poor quality (or absent) teachers. One study found that spending 50 cents (32p) on treating children for intestinal parasites in Kenya increased school attendance more effectively than building new schools as children infested with worms were too ill to attend school. It cost 25 times as much to build a school as to treat all the children in a community. In Mexico, paying parents a stipend if their children attended school increased attendance by 85 per cent as it compensated the parents for the fact that the children were no longer earning money.

Five billion to one (billion)

In the mid-20th century, around one billion of the world's population were reasonably well off, while five billion lived in poverty. That situation has reversed,

> *'We have enough on the planet to make sure, easily, that people aren't dying of their poverty. That's the basic truth.'*
> Jeffrey Sachs, director, Earth Institute, Columbia University

with many countries that were previously very poor, including China and India, rising as economic powers. Now, most of the world's population live in relatively prosperous countries, with just one billion living in the worst conditions. For these people, though, standards of living have deteriorated over the last 40 years. This is often because bad governance, poor infrastructure and military conflict or civil unrest have made it even harder to distribute aid to them effectively.

Smart aid

While Easterly believes aid does more harm than good, and Sachs, with his Millennium Villages Project, supports intensive intervention, Esther DuFlo, Professor of Economics at MIT, advocates a middle approach using 'smart aid' to evaluate and target aid interventions carefully. Citing ideology, ignorance and inertia as the main reasons that aid fails, DuFlo's approach is to carry out randomized, controlled trials of aid initiatives such as giving away bed-nets to protect people from mosquitoes and providing education subsidies. The trials should reveal which interventions work and which don't, and then aid budgets can be used most effectively.

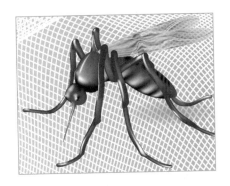

WHAT DO WE WANT, AND WHEN DO WE WANT IT?

The Millennium Goals set by the United Nations Millennium Summit in 2000 set out the eight principal goals the UN hopes to achieve through aid and other means by 2015:

- Eradicate extreme poverty and hunger, more precisely, halving the number of people living in poverty.
- Achieve universal primary education.
- Promote gender equality.
- Reduce child mortality.
- Improve maternal health, reducing death during pregnancy and childbirth.
- Combat HIV/AIDS, malaria, and other diseases.
- Ensure environmental sustainability, including limiting deforestation and cutting greenhouse-gas emissions.
- Develop a global partnership for development.

Chapter 23

How do we fare in the international market?

Improved transport and the internet have made global trading easier than ever.

It can be difficult to tell whether buying goods produced in your own country is a good idea or whether we should embrace the world market. It seems intuitive that buying home-produced goods will be good for our national economy, but it's not quite that straightforward. International trade has grown for a reason, and it can help to maximize world productivity.

Free trade and not-so-free trade

There are two approaches to international trade: **free trade** and **protectionist policies**. Free trade is trade between countries without restrictions – so with no tariffs or barriers. The opposite is a protectionist policy, which tries to protect home production by banning imports, by making them subject to higher taxes or by restricting them with a quota system. There are advantages and disadvantages to both.

If one country is very good at producing something cheaply, free trade means that it can flood other markets, stifling the local production of that good. That's fine for consumers, who can buy the item more cheaply, but bad for local producers, who might be forced out of business. On the other hand, in a protected market, consumers are at the mercy of producers who don't need to try so hard – they can sell poor quality goods at high prices and the lack of competition means consumers have no access to better and/or cheaper alternatives.

Trade and choice

One fairly obvious advantage of international trade is that it gives consumers more choice. No country has the resources and conditions to provide every possible product. Trade allows us to buy fruit and vegetables that don't grow in our climate and make things with metals not mined on our own land. Without international trade, Scandinavian consumers could never enjoy mangoes, no one in Britain could drink tea and Americans could not wear silk scarves.

Who's good at what?

The mercantile economy developed once people adopted specialized jobs rather than trying to produce everything for their own household (subsistence living), and there was increased productivity resulting from division of labour. There are good reasons for encouraging specialization in the world market, too.

Let's say one country (Italy, for example) is good at producing olives and the other (Afghanistan, say) is good at producing goats. Imagine, for the sake of argument, there are perfect trading conditions, that neither Italy nor Afghanistan is putting its resources into any other kind of production, that there are no transportation or storage costs to complicate the issue, and there is a good market for both olives and goats in both countries.

At present, both countries try to satisfy the home market for goats and olives. Their production is:

	Olives (million tonnes)	Goats (millions)
Italy	400	100
Afghanistan	200	300
Total	**600**	**400**

If Italy, which is especially good at producing olives, gave up goat-farming and concentrated on growing olives, it could increase production. Similarly, if Afghanistan gave up trying to grow olives and focused on goats, it would enjoy a veritable glut of goats.

	Olives (million tonnes)	Goats (millions)
Italy	800	0
Afghanistan	0	550
Total	**800**	**550**

(These figures are invented – please don't sell your goat/olive farm on the basis of projected rewards!)

Overall, production of both goats and olives has increased as in each country farmers are focusing on what they are good at and what their land is best suited to. Their farming is more efficient and more productive. In Italy, olive farmers have an advantage – an **absolute advantage**, as they are better at it – and in Afghanistan goat farmers have an absolute advantage because of their expertise. The two countries can trade, sharing the benefits of the improved production. The inhabitants of both Italy and Afghanistan can enjoy more olives and goats and, if there are too many, could even trade some with another country which is good at producing something different.

Who's not too bad at what?

The last example makes good sense if one country is good at producing one thing and another is better at producing something different. But what if one country is better than its trading partner at everything? Let's take two more countries, Bolivia and Brazil. Each produces only coffee and cocoa, but let's assume that Brazil is better at both than Bolivia.

	Coffee (million tonnes)	Cocoa (million tonnes)
Brazil	800	400
Bolivia	100	300
Total	**900**	**700**

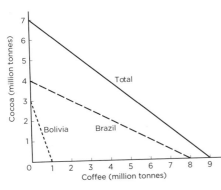

We could show the potential for each country to produce cocoa and coffee using a production possibility frontier curve (see below). Points A, B and C show how Brazil could split its resources between the two products.

Brazil could produce lots more coffee, but only if it produced no cocoa, so it has an opportunity cost in cocoa (see page 9). Brazil is twice as good at producing coffee as producing cocoa; it would have to give up two tonnes of coffee to produce an extra tonne of cocoa. Brazil has a comparative advantage in producing coffee. If we assume the profit per tonne is the same for coffee and cocoa, Brazil would do much better to focus production on coffee, which it can produce more efficiently, and trade with Bolivia to get cocoa.

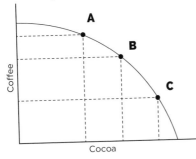

Bolivia has a comparative advantage at producing cocoa. Although cocoa production is not as efficient in Bolivia as in Brazil, it is less *inefficient*. Bolivia is *least bad* at producing cocoa, so should focus on that.

If Brazil gave up producing cocoa and Bolivia gave up producing coffee, their output would look like this:

	Coffee (million tonnes)	Cocoa (million tonnes)
Brazil	1600	0
Bolivia	0	600
Total	**1600**	**600**

This is good news for coffee drinkers, but a terrible outcome for chocolate lovers as there is now much less chocolate and much more coffee than previously. The best solution will be for Bolivia to give up producing coffee, but for Brazil to produce a small amount of cocoa to make sure the supply is sufficient to meet demand. The final production will look like this:

	Coffee (million tonnes)	Cocoa (million tonnes)
Brazil	1400	100
Bolivia	0	600
Total	**1400**	**700**

If people in Bolivia were encouraged by a 'buy Bolivian' campaign to demand Bolivian coffee, the economic situation in Bolivia would be worse, not better, as farmers would have to grow the crop they were least good at producing.

At what price?

In order to trade, the two countries need to fix a rate at which coffee and cocoa (or olives and goats) will be exchanged. Clearly, neither country will want to pay as much for the goods as it would have cost to produce them at home or there will be

no point in going to the trouble of trading, dragging goats or coffee across borders. In Brazil, one tonne of coffee is 'worth' half a tonne of cocoa (opportunity cost), which could be written as:

1Cof = ½Coc

As Bolivia can produce three tonnes of cocoa for every tonne of coffee, the equivalent expression is:

1Cof = 3Coc

The two countries will want to set terms that mean each is better off than it would have been just paying the opportunity cost to get the coffee/cocoa it wanted. They will need to fix an exchange rate somewhere between a half and three tonnes of coffee for each tonne of cocoa. In this case, 1Cof = 1Coc would see both countries better off, but Bolivia would have benefited more. They might settle on:

1Cof = 1¾Coc

because this is the midpoint between ½ and 3.

Global competition

For a country to be competitive on the global stage, it must have at least a **comparative**, if not an **absolute advantage** in several markets so that it can find trading partners. Some of what gives a country an advantage is its natural resources: Kuwait has oil reserves, Sicily has a climate suitable for growing lemons, and Iceland is surrounded by fish-rich sea. Natural advantages can change with time – new resources can be discovered and old ones can run out; climate can change. Sometimes, something previously valuable can become less valuable – just as the value of bat guano dropped as artificial fertilizers become cheaper and more efficient. A country can give itself a competitive advantage through developing its human resources with education and training or by investing in a market it wants to build.

In terms of international trade, it's best if the market being built is exportable. Iceland would not increase its international competitive edge by perfecting sledges, which are not wanted in many places, nor France by perfecting hairdressing, which can only be provided *in situ* and not exported.

That's not all

We have massively oversimplified the position of our example economies and exports to show why countries might trade. Inevitably there are other factors at play that determine whether a country will be successful at trading in the world markets. For example, Italy might reject Afghanistan's

goats as too scrawny, and Afghanis might find Italian olives too salty. There are many reasons why a country might not be competitive.

Some of these are price-related:

- **Exchange rate:** if one country has a strong currency and the other a weak currency, it will be difficult for the country with the strong currency to persuade the other country to pay enough for its goods to make the trade profitable. A strong pound/dollar/euro is bad for exports.
- **Inflation rate:** if inflation is higher in one country than another their exports will effectively go up in price (by the difference between the two inflation rates) in the importing country, making them progressively more expensive.
- **Unit labour costs:** this is the cost in labour of producing each item. If unit labour costs go up, the cost to the exporter of the item increases – passing on the cost means the item is more

expensive (so less attractive and competitive) to the importer. (If wages rise, but productivity also rises, the unit labour cost might not change, so there is not necessarily a direct correspondence between wage rates and unit labour costs.)

Other reasons, not related to price, include:

- **Quality of product:** if a country produces low-quality goods, they will be difficult to sell in a competitive market. There is a market for cheap goods, of course, but the exporter offering the best quality at a particular price point will be most successful.

- **Quality of service:** good after-sales service and prompt delivery build a reputation that attracts further business. The opposite is also true – poor service will cost business.

- **Marketing:** researching a market, making a product that meets customer requirements and advertising the finished product are important ways of creating enthusiasm in a market. A country will import goods if there is demand for them over alternatives.

- **Income elasticity:** this is the change in wealth of customers in an economy. If people in a country have more money to spend on imports – and a desire to spend the money on imports – exporters will be more successful in that market.

- **Nationalism:** people might prefer, or be encouraged, to buy home-produced goods. There might also be a preference for home-produced goods out of concern for the environment, with people trying to minimize their carbon footprint by buying goods that have not travelled far.

Trade barriers

Governments will sometimes introduce barriers to free international trade with the intention of protecting home producers. They can do this by introducing tariffs (taxes on imported goods) and imposing quotas, which limit the quantity of certain goods that can be imported. There are generally more losers than winners from a protectionist policy.

The winners are the domestic producers who, uncompetitive when faced with imported goods, are able to capture the home market. Their goods might be more expensive or of lower quality than the imports, but will still be successful if they are all that is available to consumers. The losers are consumers and the countries/businesses trying to sell goods as imports. Consumers will either have to pay more or go without – especially if the home producers can't make enough to satisfy demand.

It's also a strategy that is likely to backfire. Other countries, unable to sell their goods into the trade-restricted economy, are likely to retaliate with tariffs or quotas of their own, damaging the original country's ability to sell its own exports. In the end, the only winners are the producers of the good in the home economy (and the government in the case of tariffs, as it collects revenue). Other producers, consumers and economies all suffer.

Besides tariffs and quotas, governments can pay subsidies to a home industry to help it compete (it can afford to charge lower prices). A government can also introduce extra legislation, such as requirements for testing, that make export into the country expensive and hassle-ridden.

Agreeing to it

A **voluntary export restraint** (VER) is like a quota, except that both countries agree to the restriction. It might seem odd that a country would agree to a restriction on its exports, but it can confer a financial advantage. If the supply of a product is restricted so that there is insufficient to meet demand, the price rises. So although the exporter can sell fewer units into the market, the price of each is higher. Japan and the USA had a VER that limited the quantity of Japanese cars that could be imported into the US between 1981 and 1994. The quota was agreed because cheap, fuel-efficient Japanese vehicles were threatening the US car industry. Japanese companies began to export larger, luxury vehicles to make the most profit possible from the restricted number of sales.

Free trade or not-free trade?

Most economists believe that free international trade is the better option. It should lead, through the principle of comparative advantage, to the most efficient use of world resources. There are some arguments against it, though. Some countries want to impose trade restrictions to give infant industries (newly started industries) time to grow and find their feet before having to compete in the harsh open market. This introduces its own problems: when should support be withdrawn? What if the infant market is in fact ill-conceived and the country really has no comparative advantage in that area? How much time and money will have been wasted supporting it?

Another argument in favour of restriction is to prevent aggressive dumping of cheap goods into one country's market in order to destroy domestic competition by undercutting it. The World Trade Organization (WTO), which polices free trade, makes provision for countries to combat this.

A slightly more compelling argument is that it is perilous for a country to be entirely dependent on other economies for key commodities. They could be held to ransom by other nations, or left high and dry in a war, if they had no domestic supply of food, fuel and essential raw materials. The EU spends a great deal of its budget on shoring up the prices paid to European farmers through the Common Agricultural Policy (CAP) to prevent the food markets being entirely dominated by cheap food from outside Europe (see page 203). In an ideal world, we could assume that our trading allies would always be there with their supply of grain, gas, steel and so on – but we don't live in an ideal world.

Perhaps the most compelling argument against completely free trade, though, is that made by Oxfam, Consumers International and Friends of the Earth. They point out that although there is an overall gain to the world economy, all the gain goes to a few huge multinational business organizations. The losers are developing nations, most consumers, and the environment.

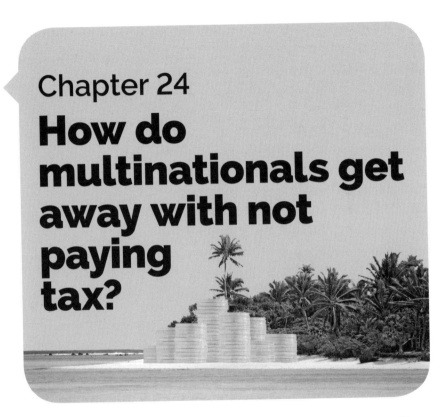

Chapter 24

How do multinationals get away with not paying tax?

Evading tax is a crime, but clever accounting can make avoiding it profitable. Globalization makes that easy.

In 2012, some major international corporations – amongst them Google, Starbucks and Amazon – faced public outrage when it became apparent that they were all paying very little or no tax in some of the countries in which they were operating.

In trouble with consumers

They were clearly doing a great deal of business, yet claimed that they were not making a profit, so did not have to pay taxes such as corporation tax. Indeed, Starbucks claimed to have been making a loss in the UK for years – at the same time as telling its investors that it was happy with the profitable UK arm of the company. The outcry led to some boycotts. Amazon was unrepentant and brazened it out. Google is quite hard to boycott as it gets everywhere.

Starbucks was easy to boycott and was the only one to throw a bone to its critics. It's quite easy to find another source of coffee, and Starbucks is, unlike Amazon, not a place for bargain hunters. Customers felt they were paying enough for their coffee and cake that they could expect the corporation to pay its due. To try to quieten protestors, Starbucks agreed to pay £20 million ($31m) to the UK tax authorities, HM Revenue and Customs, despite maintaining that it had done nothing wrong.

This £20 million ($31m) was a drop in the ocean – Starbucks had paid only £8.6 million ($13.25m) in corporation tax between opening in the UK in 1998 and 2012, despite making £3 billion ($4.6bn) in sales. It reported an operating loss every year and claimed the company would not make a profit until 2017.

Most of us would ask why, if a company has 500 coffee shops, it makes no profit? Or, if it has 500 coffee shops and makes no profit, perhaps it's not very good at the coffee business. Clearly Starbucks is pretty good at the coffee business and was not breaking the law, so how do they do it?

That'll be $4,000 (or £2,600)...

An international corporation can organize its business in such a way that on paper it makes most of its profit in the jurisdictions with the lowest rate of taxes on profit. That can be a legitimate country, such as Belgium, or a tax haven, like the Cayman Islands, that does very little other than hide money for people. (Can you think of anything labelled 'made in the Cayman Islands'?)

Let's assume an imaginary business called Quickbuck has set up a chain of shops all over Europe. Within Europe, some countries have much lower rates of corporation tax than others. In the UK, the corporation tax rate in 2012 was 24 per cent. In the Republic of Ireland (Eire), the rate is 12.5 per cent. It would obviously be to Quickbuck's advantage to make their profit in Ireland, rather than the UK, as they will pay a lot less in corporation tax. But Ireland is a tiny country, smaller than most other European countries, so even if Quickbuck opened lots of shops there, they couldn't make most of their European profit there. So they employ a nifty trick called **transfer pricing**. This consists of selling or licensing goods to themselves, from the tax haven country, for a hugely inflated price.

To do this, Quickbuck registers its logo in the Republic of Ireland and makes all its associated companies in other European countries license the logo at a hugely inflated price. There is more. Quickbuck insists on all its shops in Europe using (say) a particular type of pricing gun, which it sells to each shop at £10,000 a piece, even though they could be bought for £50 locally from a normal supplier. So the genuine profit of the other European stores is gradually eroded, squandered at the Irish headquarters of Quickbuck, where it will be taxed at only 12.5 per cent.

Bad or not?

What Quickbuck is doing is not illegal because the other European countries haven't regulated against it. (They could do – and some nations, including Japan, have in the past had quite stringent regulations preventing transfer pricing.) So Quickbuck is doing nothing wrong? Well, that's a moot point. It's doing nothing illegal. Wrong is an ethical issue, and there are no hard and fast ethical rules agreed by everyone.

The argument for saying it is wrong is that Quickbuck is benefiting from the goods and services put in place using taxpayers' money (the infrastructure, for example) but is not contributing. It is costing the taxpayer money by, for instance, damaging the roads with its large lorries, but making no contribution to the coffers. Quickbuck will argue that it's providing employment and contributing to GDP. But all businesses are doing that – and they're contributing to the infrastructure as well, so that's not a good answer. Quickbuck can be more competitive because its tax bill is lower. It can draw trade away from the companies that are paying their fair share. Is that good business sense or unethical exploitation of a loophole? Or both?

Big losses

It might sound as though it would be a relatively infrequent problem, but it's not. An estimated $200 billion (£130bn) a year is lost to governments of developing countries through businesses using tax havens – or 'profit laundering'. (Another $250 billion (£162bn) is lost through individuals using tax havens, including for criminal activity.) The total loss to world economies is $1 trillion (£648bn). As the entire global aid budget is less than $100 billion (£65bn), it's clearly a significant sum. No aid would be needed if the tax-haven loopholes were closed. Ironically for the UK, 35 of the 72 tax havens are British dependencies, territories or Commonwealth members, yet the UK is one of the big losers in profit laundering.

Doing business with yourself

There are other tactics that Quickbuck can use to reduce its tax liability. It can sell goods to itself at very low prices to move goods into an area where there is low corporation tax and it doesn't mind making a profit. It can also lend money to itself in different countries, charging itself a huge rate of interest, as a way of moving money into a low-tax jurisdiction.

The UK government believes that 50–60 per cent of all world trade is between subsidiaries within the same umbrella company, giving plenty of scope for profit laundering. Among the examples of pricing designed to take advantage of different tax rates are TV antennae sold out of China at US$0.04 (£0.025) and American bulldozers at $528 (£342). Overpriced items include German hacksaw blades, at $5,485 each (£3,556) and Japanese tweezers at $4,896 (£3,174).

Fairness triumphs

Consumer pressure and government intervention have made a difference and multinationals are being called to account. In 2012, the UK government investigated and interrogated Amazon, Starbucks and Google and lambasted them for being 'unjust', 'immoral' and spouting 'unacceptable nonsense' in testimonies to the Public Accounts Committee. The EU's Taxation Commissioner has proposed closing the loophole that allows large multinationals to use 'aggressive tax planning'. In advance of changes in legislation, the prime targets of public criticism have begun to pay more tax in the countries in which they operate. The US tax authorities have asked Amazon for a back payment of $1.5 billion (£970m).

PICTURE CREDITS